Cookery for Maids of All Work
by Eliza Warren

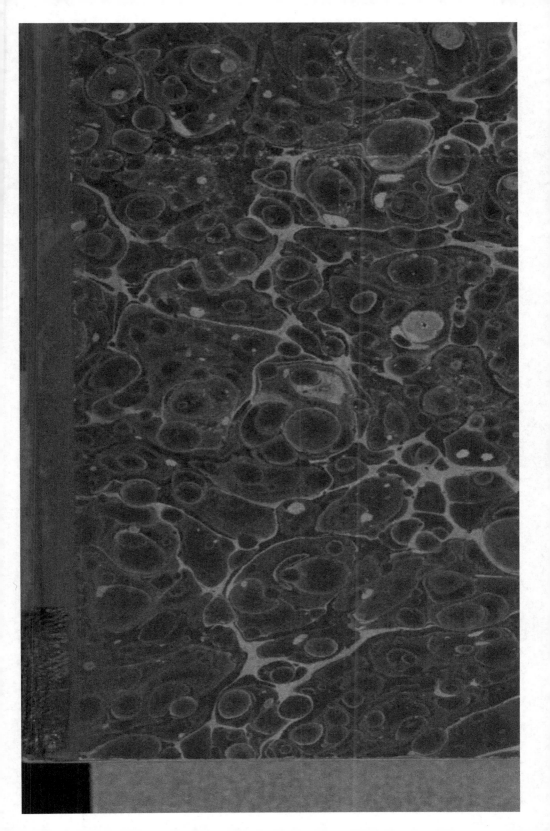

600070629U

600070629U
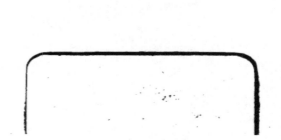

COOKERY

FOR

MAIDS OF ALL WORK,

BY

MRS. WARREN,

Editress of " Drawing Room Magazine," " Books of the Boudoir,"
" Timethrift," &c.

A GOOD SERVANT WILL NOT REPLY TO A MISTRESS, NOR
LISTEN TO EVIL THINGS SAID OF HER.

SAUCY ANSWERS DO NO GOOD.

LET SILENCE BE THE BEST ANSWER A SERVANT CAN MAKE.

UNDER ALL CIRCUMSTANCES NEVER UTTER AN UNTRUTH.

BE HONEST IN DEED, BE HONEST IN WORD.

DRESS ACCORDING TO PLACE, AND AS THE FUTURE WIFE OF AN
HONEST WORKING MAN SHOULD DO.

LONDON:
GROOMBRIDGE & SONS, 5, PATERNOSTER ROW;
ALL BOOKSELLERS, AND RAILWAY STATIONS.

1857.

TABLE OF CONTENTS.

INDEX.

ADDRESS.

Much of the comfort of numerous households depends upon that very useful person, the "Maid of All Work." Yet she is generally found to be totally unfitted for her situation both by education and habit. Being early sent from home to gain her own living, she first of all gets a place to drag children about, then as time goes on, to help a little in the house, then to do a little washing—to cook after a fashion—and she then begins to look out for a better place, asking high wages, and professing to be a good plain cook, though she does not even know what it means, never imagining it is to cook a plain joint and vegetables well, and as well as the first cooks in the land can do it. Thus she disappoints her mistress; but if that mistress would enquire previous to engagement how the intended servant cooked any articles of food, such as to fry fish, or to boil a leg of mutton, there would be much less disappointment; as a mistress must know that if a servant cannot clearly describe in what manner she would set about cooking a particular article, neither can she perform it. Cookery is no random art to be acquired by guessing, and though its rules are simple, they must be rigidly followed. Many girls really desirous of becoming all they profess to be—plain cooks—procure some cookery book and think their difficulties are overcome, when to their dismay, the first dish they proceed to cook therefrom, they are stopped in the very outset; it may be to boil— whether the water is to be used hot, cold, or boiling, is never mentioned, yet in this very circumstance is the whole mystery. Again the extravagant materials directed to be used either of quantity or quality, effectually deters the mistress from following up the instructions, and but too frequently, the poor mistaken girls, not knowing the cost of articles, scarcely conceal their contempt for an employer who will not afford such things. Such girls will in all probability become the wives of poor men, and *poor* indeed they will keep them all the days of their lives. Let a mistress once make them understand, that food can be well cooked without all these aids, and show them the way in which it can be done, that order, neatness, cleanliness, and regularity, will be insisted on—then, indeed, is part of her woman's mission on earth well performed, for she not only brings comfort to her own family, but teaches others the way to make a pleasant home, a contented husband, and healthy children ; teaches them to make their provisions go farther, and their earnings to bring greater comfort. It is to such a woman that the words of the Preacher may be applied, " Her children arise up and call her blessed, her husband also, and he praiseth her."

To be a help to the helpless, and of a little assistance to young mistresses, has been the aim of the writer. The recipes are not taken from any cookery book, but have been for many years tried in her family, have been written on slips of paper from experience, and given to servants who have never cooked before, and where the directions have been rigidly followed, have never failed.

The phraseology and cooking terms have been carefully adapted to the comprehension of servants; all long and scientific words avoided; and, as much as possible, simple, but expressive words used.

GOSSIP TO YOUNG MISTRESSES WITH ONE SERVANT.

IF POSSIBLE, think over-night what will be required for the next day's dinner, so that the servant on taking away the breakfast things, may know what she has to cook, at what hour to dine, and how many persons she has to prepare for ; also her household work for the day, and in what manner it is wished to be done. See to the larder and its contents, or if unwell, have the remnants of food brought to you.

If possible, never send the one servant on errands—time is wasted—the affairs of the family are exposed, the ends of conversation are picked up, twisted into something impossible, and you are remarked in the neighbourhood as having said or done this or the other, of which you know nothing. It is much better to let tradesmen call, or order all things yourself.

If possible, send a servant to bed at ten o'clock ; let her rise at five o'clock in the summer, and six in the winter ; make no agreement to call her in the morning, but distinctly decline to do so. Place an alarum clock in her room, which will cost but a few shillings, and hold her *in a measure* responsible for its getting out of order ; otherwise there will be constant complaints of its either going too fast or too slow. Let it be *possible* to make a place for everything, and have everything kept in its place. Never attend to the numerous wants that some servants ask to be supplied with, be assured they are even worse than indifferent helps, as they wish to make a show of doing and understanding work, but mean to neglect it as much as they can. " Bad workmen always find fault with their tools," is a true proverb ; for good workmen will work with anything that comes to hand ; nevertheless, things proper to work with, they must have. A few words here, respecting house-flannels, may not be amiss ; that which is usually sold at the oil shops is made up from the worst of wool, therefore lasts no time ; home-made ones are much better ; lay two or three layers of old flannel together, tack them well all over with string, thread or cotton, fastening in the ends securely ; make a paint flannel in the same way, only about a quarter as large, with a string to hang it by ; give the servant a piece of old drugget or old cloth of any kind for hearth and step cleaning ; for tea and glass cloths, the very best material is the unbleached brown holland, at about six-pence the yard ; three-quarters of this makes one cloth ; five of these will last very well for a twelvemonth, and a maid of all-work should not have more ; they will be only thrown away, any girl ever so hard worked, should find time to wash three cloths in a day.

Many young house-wives find themselves puzzled to know what they ought to allow for a servant's consumption and use in a week. They should not agree to find them beer ; long experience has proved that they can work far better on tea than anything else ; it is just as economical, and they feel themselves of much more importance, and think better of their mistresses if tea and sugar is allowed them, as they can then have it whenever they like ; a quarter of a pound of tea and one pound of sugar, costs 1s. 4d. per week, without beer ; or two ounces of tea and half a pound of sugar, costing 8½d., a week with beer ; the former is preferable, besides they know that this is their own, and they will frequently deprive themselves of it to give to those belonging to them, who may absolutely need it :—thus, a quarter of a pound of three and eightpenny tea, 11d., one pound of sugar, 5d., half a pound of shilling butter, 6d., three quarters of a pound of eightpenny cheese, 6d, three loaves of bread at nine-

pence the quartern, 1s. 1½.; yellow soap, half a pound once a fort-
night, to wash their own clothes, and half a pound every week for
the use of the kitchen—including the washing of kitchen cloths—
thus the cost of a servant, exclusive of meat, milk, and vegetables, is about 3s. 8d. per week ; this added to £6 or £8 wages,
say the latter, will amount to about £17 10s. a year.   A maid
of all-work should never be permitted to carve for herself, and
a mistress should, if anything eatable is missing, ask for it, make
a point of always doing so, and after a short time nothing will
be found wanting or touched, or if it is, the time is come to part.
Never allow them to take dripping, for two good reasons—one,
that they will spoil the meat, to make their perquisite greater ;
secondly, that the dripping should always be made use of in a
house.   In respect to saucepans, tin ones are much better than
any other kind, they last a long time, are always sweeter smell-
ing, and are more easily cleaned and kept cleaner than others ;
less fire is required to make water boil in them, and if any soup or
liquor is left in for a night it is not spoiled, as would be the case
in iron, or copper saucepans ; lastly, they are cheaper and more
easily repaired than others.   Block tin is a thicker kind, and more
expensive ; the common tin do equally well, if in purchas-
ing, observe the bottoms are set in perfectly level, not concave,
or bent up into the saucepan, as this makes them burn out
quicker.   Round cocoa-nut fibre brushes, of two sizes, are the
best cleaners of saucepans, they save the servants' nails, and
prevent them scraping the bottoms with a knife.

In conclusion, purchase as much as possible at those shops
which have the reputation of selling only good articles ; respecting the quality of these, much information may be obtained from the little book, " How to detect adulteration in our
daily food and drink."   The advice there given respecting bread
and sugar it would be well to follow.

THINGS ABSOLUTELY REQUISITE FOR A KITCHEN,
WITHOUT WHICH IT IS NOT SO EASY TO COOK WITH METHOD, AND WITH BUT LITTLE TROUBLE.

Two wooden spoons, costing 2d. and 4d. ; perforated tin strainer, 9d. ; a whisk, 9d. ; scales and weights, 14s. ; fish kettle with strainer, 4s. 6d. to 6s. 6d. ; a wooden bowl and half circular chopper, 2s. 6d. Of course, all other implements and utensils for cooking are supposed to be in the kitchen for use.

REMARKS TO BE READ, AND ATTENTIVELY REMEMBERED BY A SERVANT.

Always make up the fire an hour before the cooking commences, so as to have it clear. Stir the fire as little as possible ; to stir much is always a sign that neither cooking nor saving is understood. As the fire burns hollow, fill up the places with coal; do not stir it down, or put coal on the top, as this will cause smoke ; keep the under bar quite clear, to cause a draught through the grate. Where there is an oven it must be well stirred out at every opening night or morning ; *it is the fine dust which prevents the heat from penetrating to the oven.* Let the fire come up to the top of the oven, not spread wide out; it does not need a wide fire to cook by, only a high one. After dinner, if the grate has been wide, wind it up, throw up the cinders, they will perhaps last till tea-time. Always keep boiling water ready. Never throw water over a grate that is hot, or it will cause it to crack.

Put bacon always in a cold pan to fry; if it is hot at first it will brown it. Save all bacon fat; it is better than anything for stuffing (suet in stuffing gets cold and disagreeable); it is excellent for frying fish, or dripping poultry. Always drain the fat from bacon by putting it on a plate before placing it in the dish in which it it to be served, which should only be done the last moment before sending to table.

All lard or dripping will use twice over, if poured while hot, into a basin of water.

In boiling an egg, it is better to put it into cold water, and take it up the minute it boils up fast, or place it in boiling water, steaming it over the steam for an instant before putting in, to prevent cracking, then letting it boil three minutes and a half.

In opening puddings, after taking off the cloth, run the knife between the edge of the bason and paste; let it stand for a few minutes, for the steam to escape, or this steam will burst the pudding, which should be sent up whole; place the dish upon it, turn it upside down, then gently shake it out into the dish. A fruit pudding should always have powdered sugar over it.

Let all cooking utensils be kept very clean; which, after washing *while hot*, should be well wiped, and placed before the fire to dry. *Never leave any dirty; they will be sure to be wanted when there is no time to clean them.*

Suet will keep a long time if every bit of blood and meat is taken out, and the suet well rolled in flour.

In conclusion, use your best ability to please; *and act by your mistress as you would have her act by you; and remember, that in all your doings the eye of God is ever on you.*

DINNERS.

*Any fish may be added to the above; if boiled fish, use roast
meat: if fried, either roast or boiled.*

DINNERS.

BOILED LEG OF MUTTON—CAPER SAUCE—MASHED TURNIPS—POTATOES—PIE, TART, OR BAKED APPLE DUMPLINGS.

THIS should be boiled in a deep fish kettle with a strainer at the bottom to take it up by, as a fork should never be stuck in the meat. Weigh the mutton, place it in *scalding* water enough to just cover it; *after it bubbles,* allow a quarter of an hour to every pound it weighs, and eight minutes to every half pound. Never allow it to boil, but just to bubble; *if it boils, the meat will be hard—if it does not bubble, the meat will eat raw.* Scum it two or three times. The *moment* it is done, lift up the strainer with the meat on it; set the strainer and joint aslant over the steam of the fish kettle at a little distance from the fire, cover with a dish cover, and a cloth over that again, to keep very warm while the dishing up of the vegetables goes on. Afterwards pour the liquor into a clean pan, set it by till next day. *The reason why meat should be placed in scalding water is, that if placed in cold water the gradual heat for so long a time till the water boiled, would draw out the juices of the meat, which the scalding water* SETS *just sufficiently to prevent the meat becoming hard.*

A Neck of Mutton will take half-an-hour to the pound.

To BOIL TURNIPS.—After washing and paring; for mashing, cut them in thin slices—for unmashed, cut them in halves, well wash, drain, and to be certain they will be a good colour, throw them into plenty of *boiling* water in another saucepan, with a small table spoonful of salt : make them boil quickly. A quarter of an hour to half an hour, according to whether they are young or old, will dress them ; then drain them into a colander, squeeze dry with a small plate, turn them into a basin, beat them with a *wooden spoon*, add *white pepper* (it is likely they are salt enough), and a bit of mutton dripping, half the size of a walnut. If there are no drainers to the vegetable dishes, place in the dish instead, a small saucer or cheese plate turned upside down. By doing this, whatever water remains in them will run off into the bottom of the dish. On this saucer mould the turnips smoothly with a spoon, then place the dish in the oven, or before the fire, for a few minutes, till the turnips are very hot ; then cover closely and send to table.

CAPER SAUCE.——For one butter-boat use a piled tea spoonful of capers, for a sauce tureen use two. Chop them fine on the back of a dinner plate—not on a board, as the flavour runs into the wood. When chopped place them in the sauce boat with a tea spoonful of the caper vinegar (replace this vinegar every time in the bottle by adding fresh). Then, TO MELT BUTTER, if for a sauce-boatful, measure one and a half of the sauce-boat of cold water into a jug, take in a basin two tea-spoonfuls of flour and a small pinch of salt ; gradually mix the cold water with the flour till quite smooth ; put two ounces of butter into a very clean saucepan, then *strain* the mixture of flour and water on the butter, set it on a slow fire, keep shaking it one way till sufficiently thick, but not allow it to boil, as that would thin it. Take out three table-spoonfuls into the basin, *strain* the remainder on the capers, and pour backwards and forwards twice or thrice. Place this in the oven, or close to the fire, to keep hot. Take two spoonfuls of the mutton liquor, mix with the three table-spoons of butter, shake it well together, and pour hot over the mutton. Let all be as hot as possible, including the plates ; and be careful that the bottoms of these, as well as the dishes, are well wiped before bringing to table.

SECOND DINNER.

WHITE SOUP FROM THE LIQUOR IN WHICH THE MUTTON WAS BOILED—COLD MUTTON—BAKED POTATOES—BAKED ONIONS —APPLE FRITTERS.

WHITE SOUP. — Well skim the mutton liquor, and set the fat to drain, as this will make an excellent cake. Take a pint of liquor, put it into a clean saucepan with three large onions, skinned and cut into quarters, eight allspice corns, and the shank-bone, or any other ; let it boil fast for one hour, then strain it ; take a quart more liquor ; add a quarter of a pound of maccaroni, broken up into small pieces ; after it has boiled half an hour skin three onions, cut them across in thin rings, then chop them small ; take one head of celery, wash very clean in lukewarm water, cut these also in rings first, then chop across ; put the onions, celery, a *little* salt, and one ounce of butter to the soup ; let it boil another half hour, when it will be ready. To thicken, rub a tablespoonful of flour, smoothly, with a little cold water ; then beat a little of the hot soup with it, and strain to the other soup ; beat altogether well with a long wooden spoon ; let it just simmer ; add a tea-spoonful of essence of celery, see page 21. The full cost of this will be—Onions, 2d. ; quarter of a pound of maccaroni, 2½d. ; one head of celery, 1d. ; butter and spice, 1d.—total 6½d. It will serve six persons well ; and if a little of the cold mutton, free from fat, be minced and mixed with it, and served with a dish of mashed potatoes, it will make an excellent dinner.

TO MASH POTATOES.—When nicely boiled or steamed, but not too much broken, first set the dish they are to be served in to warm, either before the fire or in the oven; then turn the potatoes into a large white basin or pan, and with a wooden spoon beat each potato against the side of the pan till soft, which must be done quickly or they will cool. When all are well bruised, with no hard bits remaining, add to three pounds of potatoes two small table-spoonfuls of milk, and a little salt, beat well together, then press hard and round into the bottom of the pan, till about the size of the dish they are to be sent to table in; then place the dish on the top of the pan, turn the pan upside down, and they will fall in a round form into the dish. Rub a very small bit of butter over the potatoes, score them across the top with a knife, set them slanting before the fire, or place them in the oven to get hot and brown. If parsley is plentiful, a little wreath of this round the dish looks pretty.

TO BAKE POTATOES.—Wash them very clean in slightly warm water with a brush, to get the dirt out of the eyes, wipe dry, set them against the side of the oven, but not that the skins will burn, turn them round once or twice; from an hour to an hour and a half, according to the heat of the oven, is sufficient time for them; but if they cannot be served, which they should be, directly they are done, set them in a cooler place in the oven, and unlatch the door of the latter, but not set it wide open; upon *this* depends whether they are served to look shrivelled, or to look round and plump. A pat of butter must be sent to table with them. Cold caper sauce with cold mutton and baked potatoes is excellent; or where children are, a gravy may be made as at page 24, for beef.

CELERY ESSENCE.—Put two ounces of celery seed into three ounces of strong spirits of wine ; in a week it will be fit for use and will save the use of celery altogether.

BAKED ONIONS.—If Spanish, they should be thrown with their skins on into a large saucepan of *boiling* water, with a little salt, and kept boiling fast for an hour, then taken up, well wiped, and each onion securely *wrapped in paper* to shut out air, and baked for two hours-and-a-half keeping them well turned to the hot side of the oven. When they feel very soft through the paper they are done ; serve very hot, with the paper only taken off; unmelted butter, pepper, and salt, should be eaten with them ; or peeled, and gravy poured over.

To BAKE COMMON ONIONS.—Choose the largest, roll them well in paper, and bake an hour-and-a-half; dish up as the Spanish.

THIRD DINNER.

HASHED MUTTON, OR MINCED MUTTON, MASHED POTATOES, APPLE OR RHUBARB PIE.—Cut off the meat into slices, neither too large nor too thin, slightly pepper, salt, and flour both sides, set these on one side ; take the bones and all the sinewy pieces, but no fat, with ten bruised allspice berries and a quart of water, let them boil *fast* for two hours, then strain, and put the liquor on to boil again ; peel and cut into fine rings and chop finely one large onion, throw it into the boiling liquor for six minutes ; now thicken the liquor by rubbing smoothly in a basin one table-spoonful of flour with a little cold water, then add gradually the hot liquor, beat up well, add a tablespoonful of any sauce, if liked, return it to the saucepan, let it just bubble, then place in the meat in layers, let it stand on a very hot place till warm through, *but it must not boil, or even bubble, or the meat will be hard ;* ten to fifteen minutes will warm it through. Take a round of toasted bread (or more where children), cut it first into eight squares, then across the squares, so as to make sixteen three-cornered pieces. After pouring the meat and gravy into the dish, set these round in vandykes; serve very hot. Or if hash is wanted immediately, melt a little butter water, flour, and salt, free from lumps, when it simmers, and is sufficiently thick, put in a tablespoonful of Reading Sauce, slightly flour and pepper the meat, put it in, let it simmer up once, *not boil*, serve with bread as above.

MINCED MUTTON, EQUAL TO VEAL.—Cut off the meat, free it from sinew, skin, and much fat; boil the bones with these pieces and allspice, as before directed, and a little lemon peel, if liked ; strain, and when thickening the liquor, use a good tablespoonful of flour, and a piece of butter the size of a walnut ; no sauce. Have the meat minced not so fine as for mincemeat, still it must not be large ; add a little salt and grated nutmeg, put it in the liquor, and manage it as directed for hash—that is, *not let it boil.* Or if wanted before gravy can be made, prepare it exactly as for quickly-made hash.

FOURTH DINNER.

ROAST OR BAKED BEEF — YORKSHIRE PUDDING — GREENS, BROCOLI—BUTTERED PARSNIPS OR CARROTS—POTATOES—HORSE-RADISH—SULTANA PUDDING.

Beef, whether roasted or baked, will take either fifteen or twenty minutes to the pound, according as a family may like it much or slightly done; at fifteen minutes the red gravy will be in it ; at twenty minutes it will be dry ; but whatever the weight and time allowed, fifteen or twenty minutes must be reckoned extra, to let the meat warm ; exactly as in boiling meat, the time is reckoned from the period it BOILS, *and not from the time of putting in.* First, if to be baked, flour the meat well, and if fat, let a good tablespoonful of flour be scattered over the dripping pan (this will brown and make gravy). The meat should be turned round three or four times during baking, and should it require, flour it again; also open the oven door frequently, to let out the steam. When done, take up, and set in a warm dish on the top of the oven, cover close (and in this state it will not hurt if kept for an hour).

To MAKE GRAVY.—Some persons only like to have the dripping taken away and merely boiling water, in which a little salt has been dissolved, poured over the meat. Of course much cannot be made in this way; and where children are, a great saving of meat is effected by pouring off the dripping, all but about a tablespoonful. Take two teaspoonfuls of flour, a little salt; mix smoothly in this dripping, rubbing the brown flour up with it; then add gradually hot water till sufficient is made; set the dripping pan over the fire a few minutes—*not let it boil;* add a little colouring as under, then pour over the meat. This is nutritious and wholesome; the flour here absorbs all the fat.

BROWNING FOR GRAVIES.—Take two pounds of treacle, set it in an oven for two hours till it boils, and becomes nearly black; then take it out, and, while hot, stir into it two tablespoonfuls level, of grated salt, three of vinegar, and five of hot water; stir it frequently till cold, then bottle. This will make a full pint of browning, and will cost 8d.; or burn a little sugar in an *iron* spoon, and pour water over.

FOR ROAST BEEF.—Set it some distance from the fire at first, placing it gradually nearer after the first quarter of an hour, which time must not be reckoned. Drip it frequently;

twenty minutes before taking up, salt it slightly ; flour it well, and as it browns, flour again ; take it up, pour off all the fat ; burn in an iron spoon a little moist sugar, then pour sufficient boiling water over the burnt sugar into the gravy; or use colouring ; then pour it round the meat, *not over it.*   If a sirloin be chosen as the joint, and the family is small, cut off the meat that turns over at the end ; salt it by well rubbing salt into all the crevices as well as over the surface of the meat ; this will make an extra hot dinner, or make out with soup from the bones of the joint. *To dress this,* wash it first in a little warm water; place it in cold water; boil it very gently one hour and a half from the time it boils (that is supposing it to come off a joint of eight or nine pounds), serve it with boiled rice round the dish ; or gravy made from one half liquor it was boiled in, a little melted butter, and a dessert spoonful of made mustard to be well rubbed in with the liquor and butter, then poured over it ; serve carrots in a separate dish.

UNDER CUT OF SIRLOIN.—If it is not much prized at dinner, will make into a hot dinner for one or two persons, or as a breakfast dish.   If for dinner, cut into thick slices, then broil on gridiron (but this, only a good cook can perform well), keeping the slices turned every minute, then having a very hot dish which has been well rubbed over with eschalot or in which a small spoonful of Reading, or other sauce, with a lump of butter the size of a walnut has been melted before the fire ; take off the steaks without sticking the fork in them ; turn them in the gravy quickly, cover close ; broil some small slices of fat, take up these on to another plate, let them stand to drain a minute ; pepper and salt slightly the steaks, then place one piece of fat on the top of each steak ; send to table very hot.   This broiling requires great care and a very clear fire.   Frying will almost do as well if properly done.   Into a clean pan shred up some suet

or beef fat; when it *boils* put in the steaks and turn them frequently, never allowing the side next the pan to get hard, or it
will be spoiled; when done, take them out on a clean hot plate to
drain all fat off; then put them into another hot plate with
sauce, as before directed, or serve with only a little butter,
pepper, and salt.

YORKSHIRE PUDDING.——Take two eggs, a pint of milk or
water, half a teaspoonful of salt, beat well together, put six
ounces or six piled table spoonfuls of flour into a basin, gradually mix the eggs and milk with it into a smooth batter, and
beat it altogether for a quarter of an hour. Place the meat on a
stand over this to bake, or under the meat to roast. *Where there is a
family, it is desirable to have plenty of gravy, which is lost if this
pudding is baked under the meat.* It is equally good if baked
as follows :——Rub a tablespoonful of beef or mutton dripping
(as the joint may be) over the bottom and sides of an oval
dripping-pan, twelve inches long and eight wide, pour the batter
through a strainer into the pan (should there be any lumps, these
can be beaten smooth in the strainer); bake an hour-and-a-half,
keeping the pan frequently turned round, to brown the pudding.
Serve it on a very hot dish, cut into sizeable pieces for helping,
and let it be the last thing put on the table. Or, bake it under
the roast meat for the same length of time, turning it as above
directed. A pudding made as above, with some peppered short
bones of a neck of mutton, breast of veal or mutton, and some
chopped onions stirred in, will make a good, cheap and relishing
dinner with plenty of potatoes.

To BOIL CARROTS.——Winter carrots only should be used
with beef. Scrape and wash them very clean; do not cut them
in halves, but cut off a little of the thick end and the extreme
point (these can be boiled at the same time, but should be

reserved for the soup to be made from the bones) ; place the carrots in cold water, with a little soda the size of a small bean, let them boil two hours and a half ; if they should be done before this, they may be taken up and set on one side till wanted ; then plunge them into boiling water (be careful to let them be quite dry before sending to table), arrange them nicely in a hot dish, and they will look like fresh carrots newly pulled from the ground.

BUTTERED PARSNIPS.——Pare, wash, and cut in halves, throw them into boiling water with a little salt ; in twenty minutes or less they will be done ; take up, mash well, as turnips, taking out all hard pieces ; add a piece of butter the size of a walnut, salt to taste, and white pepper ; place them in a round mass in a dish, cut in diamonds across the top, set the dish in the oven or before the fire to re-warm, and serve very hot.

CABBAGE, BROCOLI, OR SPROUTS.——These are to be used in summer, the parsnips and carrots in winter. Take care that the water boils fast for an hour before the dinner is to be served. Wash the greens well *in warm water* not too hot, each cabbage or brocoli, or a handful of sprouts singly ; then throw them directly into a pan of cold water, each handful singly, as they come out of the warm water ; then, when all is in the cold water, wash well and change to another cold water ; let them remain in this till within an hour of the time to boil them ; then place them to drain, either in a clean tea cloth or a large colander, so that they are nearly dry ; then, having a *large* saucepan of water, which must boil "galloping," or as fast as possible, throw in a good table-spoonful of salt and a bit of soda the size of a small horse bean ; then put in the greens, stir them down into the water, cover the saucepan close, and make them boil as rapidly as possible by getting a good flame under the saucepan. If this is not done the greens will be tough, of a bad colour, and very indigestible. Summer cabbage takes ten to twelve minutes *after it boils; young heads of brocoli,* eight to ten minutes; *brocoli sprouts,* the same *when picked off the large hard stem; sprouts of greens and Brussels' sprouts,* ten minutes; *turnip greens,* five minutes; *white-heart hard cabbage,* when boiled half an hour, take up and plunge it into a fresh boiling water with salt and soda; let it boil another half hour. *Young Savoy plants* take ten to fifteen minutes; *old Savoys,* twenty to thirty minutes. With all greens or vegetables whatever, the instant they are done sufficiently, they must be taken up quickly into a colander, some of the water poured out of the saucepan, the colander placed on the top of saucepan, with a plate on the greens; if brocoli, the cover of the saucepan; they will thus drain well and keep hot; but be careful the water in the saucepan does not touch the bottom of the colander by several inches, or the greens will take up both taste and smell of the water they have been boiled in, *and become unwholesome to eat.* THE GREAT ART IN COOKING GREENS is to have a large saucepan and plenty of *fast-boiling water,* to let them *boil very quickly after they are put in,* to take them up the *instant* they are done, and not to let them *touch* the water they have been boiled in. Washing greens in salt and water is not good. It is quite true that it kills all insects and snails, but it causes many of them to give out a slimy matter, by which they stick on to the vegetables instead of falling out. Warm water causes them to fall off instantly. But whatever helps may be suggested to save trouble, nothing should prevent a clean servant from closely looking into every leaf if possible. Soda is not injurious; on the contrary, used with cabbage, is very wholesome indeed. Though, if much is used, is apt to destroy the flavour of delicate vegetables. *Horseradish* should be well washed and placed in a dish of cold water for an hour or two before scraping.

FIFTH DINNER.

VEGETABLE SOUP FROM BONES OF BEEF; COLD BEEF; FRIED POTATOES; BREAD AND BUTTER PUDDING.——Peel and cut into rings six onions; have ready in a frying-pan one table-spoonful of dripping, boiling hot; place the onions in with a little salt, and fry of a dark brown, *but not burnt*; take ten cloves, ten allspice berries, ten black peppercorns, bruised, and one teaspoonful of essence of celery (page 21), or bruised celery seed; put this with the bones, onions, and bits of skin, but no fat, into three quarts of water; boil fast for three hours, till reduced to two quarts, or less, as may be wanted; then strain and put on to boil again; grate up the cold carrots, or if there are none, some must be put to boil when the bones are put on, but not in the same saucepan; also mince six turnips, one head of celery very fine, two onions, and if in the summer mince two lettuces; add sufficient salt and a little pepper, let it boil an hour; thicken with two tablespoonfuls of flour, rubbed smoothly in a little of the liquor, and a piece of butter the size of a walnut; bake two or three rounds of bread and slightly butter on both sides, *if liked*; set it up on end or in a toast rack to be crisp, then cut into small square bits and serve on a separate dish. Where there are children, a suet pudding which has been boiled three hours, then cut into slices, will please and satisfy *them* better than bread. This soup can be made in three hours if attention be paid to it.

SIXTH DINNER.

ROAST SHOULDER OF MUTTON; ONION OR CELERY SAUCE; POTATOES; APPLE OR RHUBARB PIE; JAM TART OR ROLLED JAM PUDDING.——This joint will take twenty minutes to the pound, with twenty minutes over for warming, which must not be reckoned; make the gravy as directed for beef, page 24.

FOR ONION SAUCE.—Half an hour before dinner is ready to be served, peel six or eight large onions, according to the size of family; wash them well and cut them into thin rings; have ready a large saucepan full of *boiling* water, throw in the onions with half a tablespoonful of salt, stir them down into the water, make them boil up very quickly, and in six or eight minutes, according whether summer or winter onions, they will be done; drain them into an earthenware colander, press the water from them with a plate or saucer, and with a wooden spoon well mash them into a pulp; flour them well and turn them into half a pint of milk; well beat, then turn them into a saucepan to make very hot, but not *boil*; no butter is required in the sauce with roast meat; only with rabbits and boiled meat. By thus cooking, there are no skins or waste, all is good, eatable, and like marrow.

CELERY SAUCE.—Wash the heads of celery in slightly warm water; pull each piece apart to free it from grit, cut into small pieces of two inches in length; throw into boiling water with a small piece of soda the size of a large pea, make it boil very quickly for twenty or thirty minutes; while it is cooking take half a pint of milk, a walnut-sized piece of butter, a good teaspoonful of flour, a saltspoonful of salt; melt it together in a smooth mass so that there are no lumps; the moment the celery is done drain it, flour it, and put it to the melted butter, letting it stand where it will only thicken and *not boil*. Both these sauces must not be touched with an iron spoon, or they will blacken. They may be served as vegetables, in a vegetable dish.

BAKED POTATOES IN DRIPPING.—Instead of baking the potatoes under the meat, by which the gravy is lessened, an excellent way is, if any potatoes have been left from the day before, to place them in a separate dripping-pan with some dripping on the top, and let them bake an hour; or boil some till they are three parts dressed, then bake them for half an hour or more in the same manner, and when done spread them on a dish before the fire for a few minutes to dry the dripping away; sprinkle a little salt over, then dish them on a clean dish; send them up hot. Instead of the hard, indigestible potatoes so often presented, potatoes in this way are mealy and of a beautiful brown colour, and certainly cannot be unwholesome.

SEVENTH DINNER.

BOILED LEG OF LAMB—PARSLEY AND BUTTER—BROCOLI—GREEN PEAS—GOOSEBERRY PIE.—All young meats require to be more cooked than older meat, therefore lamb will take twenty-minutes to each pound after it bubbles; it must be placed in a deep fish-kettle, with drainer at the bottom, in nearly scalding water, but then not allowed to bubble too quickly, or the meat will be hard; scum it well, and keep covered with water; when done take it up at the instant by the drainer, not stick a fork in it; set it across the kettle so as to be kept warm by the steam; cover with a dish cover, and a cloth over that; send it to table with a little plain melted butter over. Save the liquor in which it was boiled.

PARSLEY AND BUTTER.—Have ready a small saucepan of boiling water, pick the parsley free from stem, wash in two or three waters; press in a clean cloth, then throw into the boiling water; make it boil quickly; after this allow two minutes, then strain it off; chop it on the back of a plate, as wood sucks up the flavour, then turn it into the butter-boats, melt butter as directed for leg of mutton; strain it to the parsley, and well beat up with a fork; if parsley is plentiful boil and chop sufficient to garnish the dish, by putting six pats round the edge of the dish.

GREEN PEAS.—There are two ways of dressing these; first, let them be shelled with clean hands, not taking up the pea pods into the same dish as the shelled peas are in; wash them the instant before they are to be boiled, have ready a saucepan of fast boiling water, throw into it (for half-a-peck of peas) a small tea-spoonful of salt, a piled tea-spoonful of moist sugar, a large sprig of mint (which must afterwards be taken out) or some parsley leaves free from stem, which many persons prefer; then put in the peas, which make boil up very fast; when done, which will be from ten to twenty minutes according to age, strain, and set the colander over the saucepan, and the water which drains from them will keep them hot for a few minutes till ready to serve, then turn them into a dish, with or without a lump of butter, and serve hot.

EIGHTH DINNER.

PEAS AS ABOVE WITH BOILED BACON.—Scrape the bacon well on the rind and under part (or in the boiling this will make an unpleasant taste); put it in cold water; allow one hour to each pound after it boils, which must be slowly. When done, skin off the rind, with a clean grater grate some crust of bread over. This is a humble dish, but one that most people like. *Another way of dressing peas*—and where there are children they go much further—is to boil them with only a small quantity of water, scarcely enough to cover them, sugar, salt, and mint; the latter must be afterwards taken out. When dressed, thicken the liquor with a little flour and cold water, rubbed smoothly in a basin, a small lump of butter, or any gravy that might have been left from a previous dinner; let all simmer up *once*, but not boil. This is very nice indeed.

GOOSEBERRY PIE—For Paste, see page 71.

NINTH DINNER

SOUP FROM LIQUOR THE LAMB WAS BOILED IN—COLD LAMB
—SALAD.

Put on a quart, or three pints of the liquor, with a little mace, one
peeled onion slightly cut across, or omitted if the taste is not liked,
quarter-of-a-pound of vermicelli broken up small, a little salt;
let it boil one hour, take out the onion, beat up two yolks of
eggs in a basin, with a tablespoonful of cold water; take a
spoonful of the hot liquor, mix it gradually with the eggs;
repeat this till the basin is full, then pour into the soup, stirring
it quickly round, or it will curdle.

A MOST EXCELLENT SALAD FOR A LARGE FAMILY.—
Three white-heart lettuces, one onion, the size of a large
nut, one middling-sized cold boiled potatoe, two salt-
spoons of salt, three of dry mustard, two of moist sugar,
two hard boiled eggs, two tablespoonfuls of salad oil, two
of vinegar, one of anchovy sauce. Wash the lettuces first
in warm water, then in cold, pulling them leaf by leaf, and
saving the stalks; dry them in a cloth. In a large flat plate, rub
the salt, mustard, and sugar together, then work in the oil, so
that *it is not visible*. Rub the potato smoothly into this; shave
the onion as fine as possible, chop it finely, mix it in well; take
the yolks of the eggs, mash abroad, and mix smoothly, chop the
whites small, and mix; take the anchovy and mix in a thick
mass; lastly, put the vinegar *very gradually*, cut the lettuces
into pieces of two inches long, cutting the stem into slices, where
it is not woody, then place them in the salad bowl, or a vegetable
dish, pour the mixture over the salad, and mix altogether well;
it should not be poured over the lettuce till just before serving.
Any other salads may be dressed in the same way, excepting

c

water-cresses and small salading.   Endive, celery, and sliced
beetroot, make a good salad.

To Boil Beetroot.—Carefully wash the dirt from the outside, but take care not to bruise the skin; neither take off the
end or the top, or the colour will come out; put into boiling
water and boil four or six hours; take it up by draining all the
water from the saucepan, then take it out with the fingers, and
lay it on a dish till next day, then peel it and cut into thin
slices to mix with salad; or cut into thin slices, sift a little salt
over, then a very little vinegar, and it is an excellent substitute
for pickles.

Salad without Eggs; also with Lobster.—One saltspoon (the size of a silver one) of salt, one of dry mustard,
two *piled* of moist sugar, one table spoonful of oil, one of anchovy
sauce, one of vinegar, one boiled mealy potatoe, *cold*, and to be
mashed smoothly, a tiny onion, two small lettuces or one large
one.   Pick the outside leaves off, pare the stem, wash the lettuces free from dirt and insects in slightly warm water, then in
cold; shake them dry from the water, shred them up, not fine,
into a clean cloth to more perfectly dry them; let them remain
in this till the mixture is ready. Take the salt, mustard and sugar,
mix together on a large plate with a knife which will bend in the
blade; then mix the oil well with this, so as not to be seen, then
the mashed potatoe into a stiff paste; shred the onion as fine as
possible, chop and add it; add the anchovy sauce and mix well;
lastly, the vinegar, and mix well.   Put the lettuce into a salad
bowl or vegetable dish, pour the mixture over, then mix till all
the salad is covered.   Serve directly.   *Lobster, beetroot*, or thin
slices of veal or tongue is excellent mixed with this.   If lobster,
pull into pieces with two forks (not chop it) and mix in, rubbing
the coral which is *in the head* through a colander all over the salad.

TENTH DINNER.

ROAST OR BAKED SHOULDER OR LEG OF LAMB—PEAS—
POTATOES — FRENCH BEANS — MINT SAUCE — BREAD AND
BUTTER PUDDING.

A shoulder will take eighteen minutes to the pound, to bake; a leg twenty minutes; ten minutes may be allowed extra for the warming through, which must not be reckoned: flour well before putting in the oven, or to the fire, also half an hour before taking up. Gravy as directed for beef, page 24.

FRENCH BEANS AND SCARLET RUNNERS should have the strings on each side pared off as well as the ends, unless they are very young; they should afterwards be *sliced thin*, but boiled in plenty of boiling water with (if the beans are old, a small bit of soda) and a tablespoonful of salt; make them boil up quickly, from eight to fifteen minutes according to age.

MINT SAUCE.—Wash the leaves of mint well, place a dozen or more together folded one in the other, shred very fine then chop across till also very fine; place in the sauce-boat or tureen with a pinch of salt and a teaspoonful of sugar and sufficient vinegar not to make it too thin.

ELEVENTH DINNER.

STUFFED FILLET OR OYSTER OF VEAL—BOILED BACON OR HAM,
OR RASHERS OF TOASTED BACON — BROCOLI—POTATOES—
FRUIT PIE—OR BOILED BREAD PUDDING AND SWEET SAUCE.

If these joints are very large, they will require longer than twenty minutes to the pound, and they must be thoroughly warmed through before they are permitted to become the least brown.

To MAKE THE STUFFING.—If the family is large, take half of
c 2

a half-quartern loaf, cut all the crust and bottom off fairly, that it may be used for dinner or tea, as slices of the usual loaf would be. In this manner all the crumb is left without the slightest waste: indeed, bread ought to be cut, that there shall never be any waste: Rub this crumb of bread through a colander into a pan; take a saltspoon of salt and half the quantity of nutmeg rub it in well to the bread; chop a good handful of parsley, well washed and free from stem, also a good teaspoonful, when chopped, of winter Savory or lemon thyme, both free from stem; rub this in well; have ready some melted bacon fat, pork dripping, or milk, pour it into the bread and herbs, and knead it up into a hard lump. In a fillet of veal, stuff the part where the bone is taken out; also unskewer the thin flap, put some stuffing in, then skewer or tie it up tightly. (In an oyster of veal, which is part of the bladebone, stuff between the meat and bone.) Veal should be dripped with bacon fat, pork dripping, or lard; or if dripped with the caul usually sent with veal, it must be entirely poured off, as it gets cold and hard as soon as mutton fat. Flour well before cooking, and when done, make the gravy as for beef (page 24), if bacon fat or pork dripping has been used; if veal fat, substitute a small piece of butter instead —this will make the gravy less apt to disagree. If white gravy is wanted, use milk instead of water.

Boil Pickled Pork three-quarters of an hour to the pound, placing it in cold water. Ham, if dry, must be previously soaked from six to eight hours, put into cold water, and slowly boiled half an hour to the pound. If wanted to be eaten cold, directly it is done plunge it in cold water, when the skin will instantly peel off without trouble; *then when cold*, grate crust of bread over the top; this must also be done both to bacon and ham, if to be eaten warm. Be sure, in sending to table, that the grease does not run on the dish; let it be changed to another the instant before sending up.

Boïl Brocoli as directed at page 28.

TWELFTH DINNER.

Minced Veal—Mashed Potatoes—Fruit Pie—exactly as for minced mutton, page 23.

THIRTEENTH DINNER.

A Breast of Veal—Brocoli, Potatoes, Rice Pudding.— Of six pounds weight should be stewed in half-a-pint of water for an hour previously to roasting (the liquor must be saved for gravy, to be used instead of plain water) it will then take two hours to roast or bake; well flour it before putting it in the oven, or to the fire; drip it with bacon fat or lard, or with the caul that generally is sent with it; but this fat must be entirely removed before making the gravy; to make this, melt one ounce of butter, a teaspoonful of fiour, and half-a-pint or more of the liquor, pour the contents of the dripping pan, without fat, into the saucepan, stir it well, add a spoonful of browning.

FOURTEENTH DINNER.

Roast Pork Stuffed—Apple Sauce—Winter Greens— Brussels Sprouts—Hasty Pudding.

Any kind of joint may be stuffed. The meat of the under part of blade bone should be cut loose from the bone, the stuffing placed in this cut, and fastened in with an iron skewer. The meat from a loin should be cut at the under part (but it is always better to take this out to make sausage meat of) or cut at the thick end— the stuffing placed in the cut and skewered up. The meat from

a leg should be cut also at the under part, at the thick end, and
on that side which is always sent uppermost to table in a leg of
mutton, but which is the reverse in pork. In a neck run the knife
between the bones and meat, at the thick end, in which place the
stuffing, then skewer.

Pork takes twenty-five minutes to half-an-hour to the pound,
either to bake or roast, allowing beyond this an extra quarter-
of-an-hour to warm through. Well flour it before baking
especially. Make the gravy as for beef at page 24.

FOR THE STUFFING FOR PORK, DUCKS, AND GEESE.—Dry
sage is better than green, if dry it can be rubbed and
sifted through a tin strainer or sieve; if green, put a dozen
or more leaves together one in the other and shred them
finely, then chop them across the other way, till fine; peel
sufficient onions, throw them in cold water, then cut them
in thin rings, that is, across the onion; have ready a saucepan of *plenty* of boiling water in which throw a little salt
with the onions; let them boil up quickly for *two minutes* only;
drain them through a colander, and chop finely (if bread is
liked, add one third grated bread; but by this process the onions
are so mild that bread is unnecessary); now take the onions,
sage, a little pepper and salt to season, mix it well and stuff the
meat, or duck, or goose.

APPLE SAUCE.—Pare the apples and cut into thin slices up
to the core, so that the core is left in a little round stick (there is
less waste this way; put two tablespoonfuls of ale, cider or water,
and let them boil in a *tin saucepan* quickly; the sauce should be
done in a quarter of an hour; do not mash with an iron spoon,
(as iron turns all fruits black), add a little sugar to taste, and
send up hot.

Brussels Sprouts.—Wash in warm water, then cold ; then throw into plenty of boiling water with some salt and a piece of soda the size of a small bean ; boil up quickly from ten to twenty minutes. Savoy cabbage the same.

FIFTEENTH DINNER.

BOILED BRISKET OF BEEF—SUET PUDDING—CARROTS— POTATOES—SAGO PUDDING, BAKED.

Wash the meat in slightly warm water, put into a fish kettle with drainer under, and sufficient cold water to cover, let it boil up quickly, *then very slowly* ; reckoning after it boils half an hour to the pound ; in taking up lift it with the drainer, not stick a fork in ; serve either with a little of the liquor thickened with flour (free from lumps) poured over, or plain melted butter, with the carrots round the meat. A Silver side or part of the round must be put in cold water, when it boils reckon twenty minutes to the pound ; simmer slowly.

Suet Pudding.—For a family, take twelve ounces of flour, and six ounces of suet, chopped very fine, a saltspoon level of salt (or for a very good pudding, use ten ounces of flour), mix suet, salt, and flour together, add sufficient cold water to make it a hard paste, then roll out with rolling-pin, then work up with the hands into a ball, push it hard into a bason well rubbed with dripping, tie it down with a wetted, well floured cloth, put into boiling water, after it boils up reckon three hours till done ; where it is preferred without a bason, simply by tying it in a cloth, one hour and a half is sufficient ; but by putting it in a bason, it turns out handsomer-looking, and is better eating, as the *goodness* cannot boil out.

Carrots, Winter and Summer—Should be well washed, then

scraped, *then washed again*, and put in with the beef. Winter carrots will take two-and-a-half hours after they boil; summer carrots half-an-hour, placed in boiling water. For apple fritters, see page 74.

SIXTEENTH DINNER.

STEWED RUMP OR BEEF STEAK—CARROTS—TURNIPS—POTATOES
—RICE PUDDING.

The directions are for two pounds. Take four, six, or eight onions as the flavour my be liked, peel, and cut them across in rings; take two or three carrots, scrape and wash clean, cut them into thin slices across; make a frying-pan hot, put in a little dripping; when boiling hot put in the meat, make it brown on each side, *but this must be quickly done;* take it up, SLIGHTLY pepper both sides, then place the meat into a saucepan, the bottom of which should hold the meat without doubling it, or placing one piece on the other. Now fry the onions and carrots in a very hot pan, and a little dripping, for ten minutes, adding a little salt; they should have taken up all the fat. Now place the vegetables on the steaks, add one half-pint of water, let all stew slowly for one hour-and-a-half, adding a very little more water as the gravy dries up, then strain off the gravy, put the meat on a hot dish, the onions and carrots round, thicken the gravy with a little flour and water, add a little browning or sauce if liked, then pour over the meat very hot.

STEWED OX CHEEK, costing 3d. or 4d. per pound, and well washed several times in warm water first, is richer and better than steaks, and for the cost of 1s., including vegetables, a dinner for three persons can be had.

To render the dish ornamental, peel and cut in slices half-an-inch thick, some turnips, then cut them across in squares, throw them into boiling water with salt, boil up quickly; in ten or fifteen minutes they will be dressed; drain through colander, but *not squeeze*, when dry put them in lumps outside the onions and carrots; but in this case the gravy must be sent in a sauce-boat, not placed in the dish.

SEVENTEENTH DINNER.

FRIED STEAKS OR CHOPS, EQUAL TO BROILED—GREENS, POTATOES—APPLE OR RHUBARB PUDDING.—Put plenty of dripping in a pan, make it *boiling hot*, slightly flour the steaks on each side, place them in the pan, over rather a fierce fire, and when nicely browned on each side, put them on a hot dish, with a little butter, pepper, and salt; or make a gravy without butter thus: just as the steaks are taken up, well flour the pan, set it over the fire to brown, add a little pepper and salt, when brown mix it smoothly with the fat in the pan, then add half a pint of water, or less, well mix, place it over the fire to thicken, *but not boil*, then pour over the meat; chop some onions very fine, and fry in boiling fat for ten minutes, drain from fat, serve in lumps on the steaks, or rub the steaks when in the pan with eschalot, also the dish. If chops, serve vegetable marrows, see page 57.

EIGHTEENTH DINNER.

LAMB OR MUTTON CHOPS IN BATTER—SPINACH AND POACHED EGGS—YOUNG POTATOES.—For two or three chops, take two table spoonfuls of flour, a pinch of salt, and sufficient *milk* to make into a thick smooth batter, pour the batter into a dish, trim some of the fat off the chops, and if wanted to look very nice, cut off a portion of the long end, so as to make them look round; fry this fat, add more mutton dripping or lard, so as to have plenty of fat in the pan, make it boiling hot, dip the chops on each side into the batter, put in the chops; when they are fried of a nice, golden brown colour, turn on the other side; when done take them up on a hot dish, let them stand to drain, and lastly, place them on another very hot dish; lay sprigs of nicely washed parsley on the top of each, and a little round the dish. Or gravy may be made as directed for fried steaks (page 41), only it must be served in a sauce-boat, not poured over the chops.

SPINACH.—Wash the spinach well in warm water twice, to free it from grit, then in cold; pick the stems off; do not use them unless very young, put it in a saucepan with a little salt, but *without water*, in fifteen or twenty minutes it will be dressed; drain it in a colander, pressing it down with a small plate; chop it fine in the colander, then place it in a small saucepan over the fire (or in a basin in an oven), with pepper and a very little butter; chop it well up together, make it very hot, have a piece of toasted bread on a dish, place it on this, cut through into sizeable pieces, and directly before serving, place the poached eggs round it.

TO POACH EGGS.—Have a small frying-pan that will hold two eggs, fill with water, make it boil very slow, break one egg into a cup, pour it as much as possible in a lump on one side the pan, then serve the other eggs the same; but should the eggs run on one side, with a knife or thin egg-slice keep the whites up so as to set the yolks in the middle of the white; when they have set about a minute, place the knife or slice gently under them to prevent sticking, then with the knife or slice throw the water gently over the top of the eggs; put a small pinch of salt over each. They are sufficiently done when only a shade of yellow can be seen through, then take each up on an egg-slice, trim nicely round with a knife, place them on the top of bacon, or on nicely buttered toast, with bacon round, or round spinach.

NINETEENTH DINNER.

VEAL CUTLETS, PLAIN OR STUFFED—BROCOLI—POTATES.

Plain cutlets should be cut into pieces, about the size of the bottom of the flour-dredger, and beaten on a board with rolling pin ; they may then be rolled in batter as directed for chops (page 41) ; or beat up an egg, pour into a flat dish, rub through a colander into another dish some bread crumbs, then place the cutlets in the eggs (on both sides) ; take each piece up singly, and lay in bread crumbs, (on both sides) ; have ready a pan with *boiling* bacon fat or lard ; bacon fat is best and plenty of it, fry quickly of a golden brown colour ; some slices of bacon may be fried with them ; when done, take up on a hot dish, but not the one they will be served on. If too much fat is left in the pan, pour it off ; for a dish of cutlets leave about one tablespoonful ; flour the pan well, let it brown, add sufficient water, stir well, let it thicken, add a little salt ; directly before serving, pour the gravy *first* into the dish ; place the cutlets in the middle, the bacon round, but the rashers should be cut to the size of cutlets ; let no gravy be on the *top* of the cutlets ; place sprigs of parsley on the top, and slices of cut lemon round the dish.

STUFFED CUTLETS.—Prepare a stuffing, as for veal (at page 35), cut a pound of cutlets into three pieces, beat with rolling-pin, place the stuffing in the form of a roll inside, roll the cutlet round tight, fasten with a small *iron* skewer ; dip in eggs and crumbs of bread ; fry exactly as for plain cutlets. In serving, take out skewers, place them with the points of the cutlets curving out from the centre of dish, the bacon between ; a fringe of parsley all round ; the gravy, as for plain cutlets, in a sauce boat.

TWENTIETH DINNER.

CALVES' SWEETBREADS AND LIVER, OR LAMBS' SWEETBREADS AND FRY—POTATOES—GREEN PEAS, OR VEGETABLE MARROWS—RHUBARB, APPLE OR PLUM PIE.

CALVES' SWEETBREADS.—If large, place them in scalding water, boil up quickly, then boil slowly three-quarters of an hour; take up, cut off all pipe, gristle, and fat that cannot be eaten; roll them in eggs and bread crumbs (prepared as for cutlets, page 43); fry in plenty of lard or bacon fat, till of a golden brown colour; put them on a dish to drain; dish them again directly before serving, with parsley round the dish. Fry the liver the same. To this make gravy as for cutlets, page 43.

LAMB SWEETBREADS AND FRY—Are fried as above, only not boiling the sweetbread first. Where there is liver, make a gravy as for plain cutlets, page 43.

TWENTY-FIRST DINNER.

OX HEART, ROASTED TO EAT LIKE HARE, WITH CURRANT JELLY —POTATOES—APPLE FRITTERS.

This is a very economical dish. It varies in price, according to the times and butchers, ranging from 1s. 6d. to 2s. 6d.; but it will make two good dinners for a large family.

Cut from the heart every particle of fat; place the heart in scalding water, let it boil up quickly, then slowly for an hour and half; then take it up, wipe it dry, particularly the hole inside; cut off all pipe, gristle, and fat; make a stuffing as for veal, (page 35) place it in the hole, and skewer it up; flour well; roast or bake it an hour and half; drip it with lard, bacon fat, pork dripping, or a little salt butter, but avoid mutton and beef dripping. When dressed, put all the gravy into a fryingpan, with a table spoonful of the fat, made boiling; then flour the pan well, let it brown, add a little salt, and when brown, sufficient water for the gravy required; let it thicken; pour over the heart; send to table very hot, with very hot plates. Currant jelly is eaten with it.

TWENTY-SECOND DINNER.

HASHED OX HEART—GREENS—POTATOES—JAM TART—CURRANT PUDDING.—What remains cold may be cut into slices and with the gravy, or a little made fresh by putting some bacon fat or pork dripping, or salt butter, in a frying pan, and proceeding as directed for roast heart; then put into a pie dish covered with another in the oven for half an hour; or make the gravy hot in a saucepan, thicken and add browning, put in the meat, let it simmer up once, not boil. Serve very hot with hot plates.

TWENTY-THIRD DINNER.

OX HEART TO EAT LIKE DUCK—SAVOY GREENS OR BRUSSELS SPROUTS IN SUMMER—FRENCH BEANS—BREAD PUDDING.—Prepare the heart exactly as for roasting; cut some onions across in rings, throw into boiling water with a little salt, boil up quickly for *three minutes*, take up and chop finely; add some finely-chopped or powdered sage, salt and pepper (no bread, unless preferred); stuff the hole and proceed to roast or bake as directed above, making gravy the same. In the winter, this is excellent. It may be hashed next day, as above.

TWENTY-FOURTH DINNER.

BOILED KNUCKLE OF VEAL—BOILED BACON OR HAM—TURNIP GREENS, OR GREEN PEAS—PARSLEY AND BUTTER—FRUIT PIE.

This must be put into cold water, but only just sufficient to cover it, and after it boils will take a full half-hour to every pound it weighs, scum it frequently ; when done let it well drain, set on a hot dish, strain the liquor into a pan set by till next day, pour PARSLEY AND BUTTER over, made thus : wash and pick the parsley from stems, throw it into plenty of boiling water, with a little salt, after it boils up *quickly*, reckon two minutes, strain, and chop on the back of a plate ; take a tablespoonful of flour, mix smoothly, with sufficient cold water for the quantity required ; if a sauceboatful, measure a sauceboat-and-a-half of water, always allow half as much water again as will be required, as the flour will take this up.   Put, to a sauceboatful, one ounce of butter, and one teaspoonful of flour, shake one way over the fire, but not let it boil, as this thins it ; then beat up the parsley with the butter, pour a little over the meat, the remainder in a butter-boat.

BOILED BACON.—Place in cold water ; after it boils, reckon an hour to every pound ; when done peel off the rind, grate some crust of bread over.

TURNIP GREENS.—Well pick and wash in warm water, then in cold, *(observe there is no worm in the middle of the stem which there frequently is in the flat-looking sprouts)*, throw them into plenty of fast boiling water, with a little salt, and a tiny piece of soda ; let them boil very quickly up, in five minutes they are done ; drain and squeeze dry with a plate, dish up in a hot dish (or keep them warm over the steam, in the colander but not touching the water, till they are wanted), they must be cut across in squares before serving.

GREEN PEAS with mint, must be boiled with a little salt or moist sugar, in but little water (and this water must be saved if soup is to be made next day), only let the water be fast boiling when put in, and boil up quickly ; they vary in the time of dressing from ten to twenty minutes ; *if very old* add a little soda, but the water then must be thrown away. In many counties parsley is used instead of mint.

GREEN PEA SOUP—SOUP FROM LIQUOR OF KNUCKLE OF VEAL.—Take off all the fat, and an-hour-and-half before wanted, set the liquor to boil, and when boiling, if two quarts, put in four tablespoonfuls of well washed rice, the white centres of two lettuces, the liquor in which the former peas were boiled, and a pint or pint-and-a-half of shelled peas; when these latter are dressed, all will be ready; thicken with sufficient flour (about two or three tablespoonfuls), and very little water, with salt, and a *little* pepper, any parsley and butter that was left, or gravy, or if not, one ounce of butter, let all be well stirred and *simmer*, not boil, for three minutes; this, with plenty of potatoes, or strips of baked bread, will make a good dinner for a family, at less than the cost of 6d. If no meat liquor add a little more butter.

WINTER PEA SOUP.—For a large tureen full of soup take a pint and half of split peas, wash them well, pouring the water off from the top, pick out the black pieces, put them into a three-quart saucepan, three hours before the soup is wanted; add half a pint of slightly warm water, one tea-spoonful of celery seed tied up in muslin, place them on a very slow fire; when they have taken up this water, which will be in ten, fifteen, or twenty minutes, according to the fire (but the slower the better) add a half pint of warmer water. Continue doing this till the peas are quite soft; in two hours they will have taken up nearly all the water they require (but at all times they must be well watched from burning). Now cut up as many onions as are liked, cutting them across so that they fall in rings, then cut them across again, throw them into the peas with two table-spoonfuls of cold dripping. Let this simmer slowly one hour, take out the bag of celery seed or use celery essence (see p. 21) then take two table-spoonfuls of flour, mix smoothly with cold water, then *strain* into a basin of soup, pour altogether back in the saucepan, stir up well, let it simmer five minutes, it is then ready.   Bake as many rounds of bread as required, let it be cut thin, and as each piece is toasted stand it upright to become crisp, then cut into strips, then into small pieces or dice.   Serve on a separate dish, unless liked to be sent in the soup.   *The reason for adding flour to the soup is, that the dripping and the water will not mix without it; and when flour is used for this purpose, fat of any kind does not disagree with the stomach, but, on the contrary, is very wholesome.   This soup cannot be distinguished from that made with meat, and will dine a family of six persons for 6d.*

ONION SOUP.—Having for three or four hours boiled some bones, take the liquor, or liquor in which meat has been boiled (let there be no fat on it) half an hour before wanted; have ready six or eight good onions, peel, wash, and cut across in rings; then chop them again, throw these into the *boiling* liquor, with a little salt and pepper, let this boil *fast* ten minutes; if possible to procure chives, mince some very small, and throw in *with* the onions; if not, use the green tops of the onions, just the moist, tender, and young part.   Thicken the soup with one or two table-spoonfuls of flour, rubbed smoothly in a little cold water in a basin; take a little of the hot soup to this, adding gradually more, then *strain* it to the soup; put in an ounce of butter, let it simmer (not boil) up once; add a tea-spoonful of celery essence (page 21).   This is excellent, but may be made richer by beating up two eggs in a basin, then putting the flour and cold water to them, then *gradually* adding the hot liquor, or it will curdle, then *strain* the whole to the soup, stirring it rapidly round.

Ox-TAIL SOUP.—Three tails will make three pints of soup. Cut each tail into three or four joints, place them in a saucepan holding two quarts, pour on them three pints of cold water, add twenty each of cloves, allspice, and black pepper corns (or half the quantity well bruised), three onions cut up, and a tea-spoonful of salt, let this *gently simmer* an hour and a half after it boils up, skimming it well during the time. The meat should now be very tender, and ready to fall off the bones. Cut the meat into small pieces, lay it on one side, strain the soup first through a tin strainer, then through a fine sieve; thicken with one piled table-spoonful of flour, mixed smoothly in a little cold water, gradually add a little of the hot soup to it till the basin is full, then pour through the clean tin strainer into the soup; let it simmer *up once*, add the meat, and two table-spoonfuls of browning, and two of mushroom ketchup. Stir well, and simmer five minutes. Send to table very hot.

TWENTY-FIFTH DINNER.

AN EXCELLENT IRISH STEW.—Take two pounds of any mutton that has not much fat, and cut into chops; ten large potatoes, peeled, washed, and cut in halves; ten good-sized onions cut across each into four rings; take a pint-and-a-half of water, half a small teaspoonful of pepper, the same of salt, and two tablespoonfuls of mushroom ketchup and mix. Fry the mutton and onions lightly on both sides; place in a small saucepan a layer of potatoes, of mutton, and onions, one over the other; now pour a little of the well-stirred mixture over; now another layer as before, then the mixture, till all the meat, vegetables, and mix-ture are used; cover close; stew over a slow fire for three hours.

HARICO MUTTON—CARROTS—POTATOES—PLUM OR APPLE PIE.—Take part of an undressed neck of mutton (not too fat),

D

carefully take out the bone, skewer the chops round; fry them in boiling mutton fat of a nice light brown, dredging them occasionally with flour; when done just through, put them on a dish, and fry four sliced onions; lay these on the chops; cut up two pared turnips and one scraped carrot into small slices with a shape-cutter, or cut them into diamonds with a knife; these put away undressed with the chops; now take the bones of the mutton, the trimmings of turnip and carrot, a little pepper and salt, and a pint of water; stew two hours; then strain the gravy to the chops and onions, and simmer very gently two hours; a few minutes before sending to table, thicken the gravy with a little flour, and add two teaspoonfuls of colouring, see page 24; garnish with alternate shapes of turnip and carrot, which previously lay in boiling water for a few minutes, also sprigs of parsley. The harico is best made the day before, to remove the fat when cold; only in that case it must not be thickened till just before serving.

TWENTY-SIXTH DINNER.

TO DRESS HALF A CALF'S HEAD AND BRAINS——PICKLED PORK, PARSLEY AND BUTTER —— BROCOLI —— POTATOES —— LEMON OR ORANGE FRITTERS.

Take out the brains; wash the head well several times in warm water; let it remain half an hour in warm water before dressing, then put it in cold water, enough only to cover; make it boil up quickly, and remove the scum; then let it *simmer very gently* for three hours; *if it boils it will be hard*. Wash the brains well, put them in salt and cold water for an hour; then put them in warm water and skin them; put them in a saucepan of cold water; let them boil up quickly, take off the scum, then simmer for a quarter of an hour; take up and chop *not too fine*; have ready three tablespoonfuls of parsley and butter made as at page 31 ; put the brains to this and gently make hot. Skin the tongue, take off the root, place in a separate (dish ; put the brains round and mix hot with parsley and butter ; serve parsley and butter in a boat or tureen. On the head place sprigs of parsley and slices of lemon.

TWENTY-SEVENTH DINNER.

HASHED HEAD—SOUP FROM CALVES' HEAD LIQUOR—SPINACH—
POTATOES—FRUIT PIE.

Take off the fat; to two quarts of liquor take six onions sliced thin, scrape and cut very thin, three carrots, three turnips cut small ; fry them in two ounces of butter till of a light brown colour ; put them to the soup ; add a head of celery cut up thin, and a little salt ; boil an hour-and-a-half ; then put a quarter-of-a-pound of maccaroni broken up small ; boil another half-hour ; the maccaroni should be very tender ; thicken, if *required*, with a piled teaspoonful of flour, rubbed smoothly in a *little cold water ; brown with a tablespoonful of browning*, see page 24.

HASHED CALVES' HEAD.—Cut up the remains of head into nice pieces ; slice the tongue ; flour a little the pieces on both sides ; take a pint of liquor ; put in it six allspice corns or a very little mace, an onion and a little lemon-peel (or not), let it boil an hour ; thicken with an ounce of butter, a piled tea-spoonful of flour, rubbed smoothly in cold water ; add one table-spoonful of sauce, either Reading, or any other of the same description ; let it simmer, then strain ; add the meat, but not let it boil.

GREEN PEA SOUP MADE FROM CALVES' HEAD LIQUOR.—Take two quarts of liquor ; boil fast ; then throw in a quart of peas, when they are cheap ; let them boil till tender ; strain and mash them with a wooden spoon in a basin; throw them back into the soup, add a little salt, mix well, then strain or not, as liked, through a sieve, but add one ounce of butter, and a teaspoonful of flour, rubbing smoothly in a little cold water; let it simmer up once.

TWENTY-EIGHTH DINNER.
PICKLED LEG OF PORK—PEAS PUDDING—POTATOES.

Put the meat into cold water; when it boils let it bubble very slowly; allow, after this, half-an-hour to every pound.

For Peas Pudding.—Tie up in a cloth a quart of split peas; leave a little room for them to swell; place them in slightly warm water; after they boil, reckon two hours-and-a-half; take them up, mash them well with a wooden spoon through a colander into a bowl; add a good tablespoonful of dripping, or a little butter, with pepper and salt; beat it up well; wash and flour the cloth; tie the peas up again very tight; place in boiling water; after it boils reckon half-an-hour; serve hot in a warm dish. This eats very well with boiled beef.

Veal Pie from Cutlets, to be eaten Cold as a Breakfast or Luncheon Dish.—Take two-and-a-half pounds of cutlets, cut into pieces without fat, and put into a saucepan with two blades of mace, a slice of lemon-peel, half-a-pint of cold water, and a little white pepper; let it stew for two hours, strain the liquor from the meat, take out the spice and peel, and put both away to cool; boil four eggs very hard, when cold, take off the shell and *slightly* chop them; mince finely three ounces of ham, lean bacon, or remains of tongue; now mince the veal finely, and mix with the eggs and ham; make a paste (as at page 71) of ten ounces of flour, two-and-a-half ounces of lard, two-and-a-half ounces of butter, with a little water; take a quart pie dish, cut out the cover of paste, line the sides and edge of dish ; mix up the mince with the gravy (first having taken away all fat), put into the dish, cover, ornament the top with leaves of paste, or any other designs, and bake one hour-and-a-half in a moderate oven.

VEAL PIE FROM BREAST OF VEAL.—Take two and half pounds of breast of veal, for a quart pie-dish ; proceed to make paste exactly as for beefsteak-pie, adding small pieces of ham or bacon instead of fat. Bake two hours and a half in an oven that will bake meat.

BEEFSTEAK-PIE.—A quart dish will take three pounds of steak ; cut it up into sizeable pieces fit for helping, and a piece of fat for each bit of steak. Make a crust of ten ounces of flour and five of dripping, butter or lard is not so well, as the paste becomes hard. Rub half the dripping into the flour, mix up with a little water, roll out very thin, put in the remainder of the dripping, in little bits, all over the paste, roll it up in a roll, then roll it out with a rolling-pin to a little larger than the top of the pie-dish, turn the dish on the paste, cut round a little larger than the dish, lay this cover of paste on one side, roll out the pieces of paste that are left, with a cutter or knife form some leaves to ornament the top of the pie, cut the pieces of paste down the middle, line the edge and sides of the dish with this, having the cut side at the edges. Pepper and salt the meat, put a piece of fat on the top of each piece of lean till the dish is full. Pour rather more than a quarter of a pint of water in, wet the edge of the paste in the dish, place the cover of paste on the top ; do not finger it, it will stick of its own weight if the edge has been properly wetted. Place the leaves in the centre of the top. Make no opening in the top. Bake two hours and a half in an oven nearly hot enough to bake meat.

BEEFSTEAK-PUDDING.—For a quart basin, two and a half pounds of steak. If onions are liked, put in a few peeled spring onions, or fry some old onions, cut into thin rings ; slightly salt the meat, cutting it up in pieces sizeable to help at table, with a bit of fat attached, or on the top of each piece ; pepper and salt slightly. Make a dripping or suet paste, as above for pie. Make the basin slightly warm, rub some dripping round, line the basin with paste, but not cut off the paste from the edge of the basin. Place the meat in layers, with onions, or leave them out. Put in half a pint of water. Now cut off the paste from the edge, about an inch from the basin. Roll this up in a round ball, press it out to the size of the top of the basin, place it over the top, fold the edge of the paste over it, pinching it up very tight. Tie down with a wetted, well-floured cloth, put it with cloth-side upwards into boiling water, make it boil up quickly—reckon from this time three hours. When taken up, take off the cloth, just run the knife round the edge of the basin, let it stand thus five minutes *to let the steam escape*, place the dish in which it is to be served on the top of the basin, and gently turn it out whole. It is the steam which bursts the pudding.

To BOIL A TONGUE FULL SIZED.—Whether fresh out of pickle or dried it must be soaked ; if pickled at home, and just out of pickle, soak three hours, if from the butcher's, soak five hours ; and if dried, soak ten to twelve hours, according to its hardness ; place in a fish kettle with drainer in *cold* water, let it boil quickly, then simmer very gently three-and-a-half to four hours; when done put it instantly into cold water for three minutes, then peel off the skin, trim it round nicely, and set it to drain, not touching it till quite cold. Before sending to table take a long strip of writing paper, about a quarter of a yard in width, double and cut it in a fine fringe, then open it and double it the reverse side, pin it round the root of the tongue.

STEWED ROOT OF TONGUE.—When a tongue is to be pickled at home, it is sold generally with the root on. Take the root, wash it several times in warm water, to get rid of the slime, blood, &c., set it in a saucepan over a slow fire, with a bunch of sweet herbs, a little salt, a small piece of mace, or a few allspice berries, a quart of cold water, let it stew gently two hours, adding a little boiling water, as it may stew away, take out the herbs and berries, then put in four tablespoonfuls of rice, and let it stew another half hour, thicken with a little flour and cold water *(this absorbs all the particles of fat)*; add a table-spoonful of browning, page 24.

TO BOIL A HAM.—If a dry ham, of ten or twelve pounds weight, soak it eight hours, changing the water frequently ; *scrub the skin well*, put it in *cold* water in a fish-kettle, with drainer under it, or pin it in a cloth and put in the copper. When it boils, which should be in an hour, allow it five hours to simmer slowly, take it up by the cloth immediately it is done, and throw it into a pan of cold water *(this plumps it, and makes the skin peel off readily)*, let it stay in the water not more than two minutes. Put it on a fish strainer to drain, peel off the skin, set it by till cold, then grate some crumbs of bread over it ; or, if to be eaten warm, grate bread over as soon as it is peeled, but it is best not cut till cold.

FRIED RIND OF HAM.—Cut the skin into very small pieces, and roll in some sifted bread crumbs ; throw into a very hot pan, and fry quickly. Lay them on a fish strainer to drain before sending to table.

DRIED PORK CHINE should be soaked two or three hours, according to its size, and boiled about the same time, placing it in cold water, only allowing it to simmer very gently.

To DRESS A DISH OF KIDNEYS.—*Skin* but not cut them at first, either for frying or broiling. If to fry, have some mutton dripping boiling hot, pepper, salt, and flour them, fry till brown on both sides (for this the fire must be very quick); then, on the hot dish on which they are to be sent up, take them up (letting them drain from the fat), and cut them open—the gravy will run out. Place them back in the pan for two minutes, to brown the parts that have been cut; then put them into the dish, with the gravy, a little butter, pepper, and salt. Send them up very hot. Or they may be broiled on the gridiron, and served in the same manner. Or a gravy may be made as for steaks (see page 41).

POULTRY AND GAME.

TWENTY-NINTH DINNER.
BOILED FOWL—VEGETABLE MARROW—POTATOES.

BOILED FOWL.—Clean out the crop and stomach, scrape the gizzard, and wash all well; wipe dry, singe the long hairs off by holding a piece of lighted paper to the fowl, cut slightly across the bony part of the leg where it joins on to the meat, press the bony parts backwards—this will draw out the cords of the leg; cut off the legs, truss the wings, stuff or not, as may be liked, with veal stuffing in the crop (see page 35); tie up in a white cloth, put into boiling water sufficient to cover, let it boil up quickly, then boil very slowly for half an hour if a middling one—three

quarters, if a large one; when done take up, place on a hot
dish, and cover for three minutes; then remove on to another.
It may then be covered with plain melted or parsley and butter
see page 31. The boiled liver, finely chopped and put in
butter, makes nice sauce.

VEGETABLE MARROW.—Choose them young and small, when
the skin will scarcely have any thickness, nor the insides any
seeds; do not cut off the stem nor pare them; put them in
boiling water, with a little salt; make them boil up quickly.
They will take from fifteen minutes to half an hour, but should
not be very soft. Have ready a toast cut in halves and
quarters. When the marrows are dressed, drain them in a
colander for a few minutes; then, directly before serving, place
them on the toast, cut them in halves and quarters, let the toast
absorb all the moisture, then pour good melted butter over, and
serve as hot as possible; or eaten with cold unmelted butter
are excellent.

THIRTIETH DINNER.

ROAST FOWL, WITH SEA KALE—STEWED MUSHROOMS—POTATOES
—BREAD AND BUTTER PUDDING.

A ROAST FOWL will take from three quarters of an hour to
an hour. To *Bake* the same.—Prepare it as for boiled fowl
(page 56), stuff, if liked, with veal stuffing (page 35), place the
gizzard under one wing, the liver under the other; drip it with
lard, bacon fat, or pork dripping; well flour it to make a nice
brown. When done, the gravy may be made exactly as for
beef gravy (page 24); or *use brown butter sauce*, to make which,
melt some butter, burn a little loaf sugar, pour boiling water
over, or put in a tablespoonful of browning (see page 24), and
a table-spoonful of Reading Sauce.

SEA KALE.—Wash in warm water two or three times, to free from grit, then in cold water; pare the stems, cut off all discoloured bits; then wash again, tie up in bundles, put into boiling water with a little salt, make boil fast, in twenty minutes it will be done. Have ready a toasted round of bread in a dish, cut into six pieces, drain the kale, place it on this, the roots all one way, pour melted butter over, serve very hot. Asparagus is dressed in the same way.

STEWED MUSHROOMS.—Peel and cut off part of the stem, place a pinch of salt on each (*if they turn black, after an hour's standing, they are good, if yellow they are poisonous*), put them in a saucepan with an ounce of butter, a table-spoonful of cold water ; let them stew ten minutes, or more, on a slow fire, drain off the liquor, thicken with a very little flour, add a little pepper, put this liquor back to the mushrooms, simmer up once, and send up hot.

BOILED TURKEY OR ROAST.—Prepare and stuff exactly the same as fowls (page 56); be careful to draw out the cords of the legs. Whether for roast or boiled, a small turkey will take an hour and-a-half, and a very large one two hours and-a-half. With boiled turkey serve oyster sauce, see (page 64), also the liver minced fine, put into plain butter. Ham or tongue, or pork chine, to boil which see (page 55). With roast turkey, serve nicely fried pork sausages, not separated if possible, and egg sauce, see (page 68). If the gizzard and liver are first boiled for an hour, and then put under the wings, they will be much softer, and the liquor will help the gravy ; any bones boiled well the *day before* and the *fat taken off before using*, will make excellent gravy, instead of using water ; make the gravy as for beef (page 24), or browned butter, see (page 57). *In drawing the inside of a turkey and the crop, be careful not to injure the liver, and that the gall-bladder does not break.* In trussing, twist the head under the wing. If the turkey be baked, well flour the baking tin, as well as turkey, and well drip with bacon fat or lard; but in putting it in the tin, turn the breast *downwards* first; do this also with poultry, as when they are turned the breast swells out again.

ROAST OR BAKED DUCK will take from half to three-quarters of an hour, clean and wash them, then cut off the points of the wings and feet, and as much of the neck bone as possible; clean these and put on for gravy, with a few sage leaves, and a little pepper and salt, for three hours, with any bones (no fat), boil the gizzards one hour, the liver a quarter-of-an-hour, then put them under the wings to roast. For stuffing see (page 38), but place the stuffing in the *body of the duck*, and tie the end and neck up tight, also tie the wings and legs in their places, instead of skewering; drip with bacon fat or lard, flour and brown well, make the gravy as for beef (page 24), using the liquor from the bones, instead of water.

ROAST GOOSE—APPLE SAUCE.—This will take about an hour and a half, a very large one still longer; it should be served directly it is done, or the breast will fall; in roasting keep this part well floured to prevent burning. Prepare and stuff it the same as a duck, only taking care to remove all the fat which is inside; it will require to be dripped very little, unless it be a very young Michaelmas goose, then drip it as for duck; but if an old one or Christmas goose, before making the gravy, take away every particle of its fat or oil. Make the gravy as for the duck—of liquor from bones, and gizzard and liver; there should be plenty of it; it will be richer if served in the same dish as the goose, but then the goose should be carved before sending to table, and the gravy poured over it. It would save much trouble and annoyance if all poultry, rabbits, and hares, were cut up previously to coming to table. Apple sauce, see page 38.

BOILED RABBITS—ONION SAUCE.—Skin and clean, wash well, lay them in warm water a quarter of an hour, to soak out the blood.   Truss them as short as possible, put them in plenty of scalding water, make boil up fast, then boil slowly for half an hour, well scum the water.   Three quarters to an hour, if large and old.   When dressed, take out the liver, chop fine, put into melted butter; cut up the rabbits before sending to table (otherwise they look somewhat like cats), and divide the heads, pour onion sauce over send also onion sauce in a tureen, or vegetable dish ; slices of lemon round the dish.   Save the liquor in which they were boiled.   Onion sauce, see page 30.

RABBIT SOUP.—An excellent soup may be made next day by taking sufficient of the liquor, and boiling down the bones and head for an hour and half, with eight allspice berries ; strain, add four tablespoonfuls of well washed rice, four or six onions cut across in rings, then chopped again; thicken with two table-spoonfuls of flour, rubbed smooth in cold water, salt to taste, and one ounce of butter, a teaspoonful of celery flavouring, see page 21, and browning, page 24.

ROAST RABBIT—PICKLED PORK.—Before a very clear, good fire it will take from an hour upwards, stuff with veal stuffing (page 35), keep it dripped well with lard or bacon fat, let it be nicely browned.   For gravy, melt together half milk and half water, two ounces of butter, a little salt, a tablespoonful of flour, and a small tablespoonful of browning, put into the dripping-pan free from fat, and mixed with the brown and gravy from rabbit, cut up the rabbit, and pour over.

PICKLED PORK—If thin and fresh out of the pickle, should be put into warm water, allowing three quarters of an hour to the pound after it boils, which must be very slowly.

RABBIT PIE.—Cut the rabbits up in joints, dividing the backs into three, chop off the bony parts of the leg and shoulders, cut open the head, take out the brains, which put in with the meat, boil the bones and head in a pint of water, for an hour, to make gravy. Make the crust as for beefsteak pie (page 53), have some slices of ham or lean bacon, pepper and slightly salt the rabbit, place it with the ham or bacon, alternatively in layers, put in the gravy from the bones, bake, in not too hot an oven, two hours.

ROAST HARE—CURRANT JELLY—PORT WINE GRAVY.—After skinning, taking out the paunch, and washing the Hare twice or three times, wipe dry, stuff the belly with veal stuffing, pressed together very hard (see page 35); sew up securely with needle and thread, baste it for a quarter of an hour, before a clear fire, with vinegar (this makes it eat tender), then wipe out the dripping pan, baste in a half-pint of milk (this prevents the skin from hardening), cut the skin at the neck to let the blood out, now baste it with pork dripping, lard, bacon fat, or salt butter, no other kind of dripping; when well basted with this, flour it well, and as it browns keep basting and flouring, roast it an hour-and-a-half, but it must have quite a coating of flour and basting on it; for Gravy, boil some bones for hours, with a few allspice berries, strain it when the hare is ready; to a pint of this gravy add a tablespoonful of browning, two ounces of butter, a teaspoonful of flour, rubbed smoothly; let it simmer up once, then add a wineglassful of port wine, or two teaspoonfuls of vinegar. Serve the gravy separate from the hare.

HASHED HARE.—Take the remains of the hare and gravy, place in a pie-dish in the oven, and a flat dish over this—in an hour it will be ready. If more gravy is required, boil the head and pieces of bone for an hour in a pint of water, with six allspice berries, strain, thicken with a tea-spoonful of flour, an ounce of butter, and a table-spoonful of browning ; then again strain over the hare, and either hash as above, or put in a saucepan for an hour on a hot place, but not letting it simmer, only get very hot.

JUGGED HARE.—Wash the hare quickly, cut it up in pieces, split the head, put all in a saucepan with six cloves, ten allspice berries, ten pepper-corns, all bruised ; a thin piece of lemon-peel, and two large onions ; *cover* with the water containing the blood which has run from the hare ; let it simmer slowly, after it boils, for two hours ; then take up on a hot dish, keep very warm, thicken the gravy as above, only using a tablespoonful of flour and two of colouring, let it simmer, then strain over the hare, and serve very hot. *A few forcemeat balls are a great improvement.* Make stuffing as for veal (page 35), to which add half sausage-meat made from pork sausages ; mix well, and make these into balls of the size of large walnuts, dip them in white of egg, and fry in lard or bacon fat ; place these all over the hare and round, *after the gravy* is poured on the hare.

PIG TO ROAST.—A small pig will take three hours to roast or bake. Take out the liver, heart, and kidneys, wash well, put these and the pettitoes, with a saltspoon of salt, into three pints of water, add a large onion cut in four, a few leaves of sage, eight allspice berries, and eight pepper-corns, bruised ; let this boil till reduced to a pint of liquor, then strain and set it on one side ; wash the pig and wipe dry. *For stuffing,* take a sufficiency of crumb of bread rubbed through a colander, a table-spoonful of sifted dry sage, and a little salt and white pepper ; make this into a hard mass with a little bacon fat, pork dripping, or butter, each of which must first be melted before the fire ; stuff this into the body of the pig, either skewer up the skin or sew up with needle and thread. If to roast, tie two skewers across the legs that they shall not fall together over the body. Now flour the pig well all over, and wipe it off again—*this is to thoroughly dry it.* Now place it in the oven or before the fire for three minutes, then well rub it with a lump of butter tied up in a double muslin bag (*this must be constantly done while the pig is roasting*). Tie paper over the ears. The skin, or crackling, and ears, must be of a golden brown colour, not the least burnt. When done, take up the pig on a dish, cut the head off, split it, take out the brains, cut the pig down the middle of the back, cut the legs off, lay them and the halves of the head on each side the pig, keep very warm while the gravy is preparing, take a table-spoonful of flour, mix with a little of the cold gravy into a smooth batter, then add it to the whole of the gravy; add also the contents of the dripping-pan, put it on the fire, let it simmer up once, then pour over the pig.

If a pig is sent to the baker's, send with it a quarter pound of butter, divided, and tied into two doubled muslin bags, and request it to be frequently rubbed with this.

PHEASANT—PARTRIDGE—GROUSE—BREAD SAUCE.

PHEASANT.—Draw it, and cut a slit at the back of the neck, to draw out the crow or crop, let the head remain on, truss it under the wing, not cut off the legs or feet, but twist them close to the body, put a lump of butter inside the body, tie it up close, flour it well, then baste it with bacon fat or lard, before a quick, clear fire, it will take forty minutes; make the gravy as for beef, (page 24), or with browned butter see (page 57); serve separate and with bread sauce.

PARTRIDGE AND GROUSE are dressed in the same manner. A partridge will take half-an-hour; grouse, twenty minutes; both should have gravy made from bones, enriched with a little butter, and served with bread sauce; port wine gravy may be used if liked.

BREAD SAUCE FOR GROUSE.—Take a pint of milk, put into it a pinch of salt, and six allspice berries, when it boils cut a small onion in six pieces, throw in, let it boil eight minutes, then strain the liquor to a half a pint of bread crumbs, which have been rubbed through a colander, then put in a piece of butter the size of a walnut, let this gently boil for half-an-hour, beat up well, serve in a tureen with ladle.

FISH.

BOILED COD AND OYSTER SAUCE.—Cod are in season from the beginning of December to the end of April. The gills should be very red, and the flesh white and firm. It should have salt well rubbed into it, even if only an hour or two before cooking ; place it in scalding water in a fish kettle with drainer ; put in also a small pinch of salt and some horseradish (this gives flavour); after the water boils, let it bubble very slowly, so as scarcely to be seen. A small fish will take about twenty minutes after the water bubbles; a large one half-an-hour or longer. If it is carefully lifted up on the drainer, it can be seen whether it is sufficiently done ; the fins will just break away. Garnish the dish with parsley, sliced lemon, the roe and liver.

OYSTER SAUCE.—Cut off the *beards* of the oysters (the *beard* is the black frill part which is round the oyster); take these and boil them in a very little water for ten minutes ; strain this into a basin, also the oyster liquor ; mix a tablespoonful of flour smoothly with a little of the liquor *when cold*. Strain to three ounces of butter or less, according to the number it is to serve ; add more water if required ; let this simmer, then add the oysters, and simmer three minutes ; beat up a spoonful of Harvey or Reading sauce with it if liked.

HASHED COD.—If any fish is left, take it out in flakes while warm ; next day melt some butter, place the cod in it, and gently shake it round once or twice till hot ; garnish with parsley round. This is really nicer than on the first day.

TO BOIL SALMON——ANCHOVY SAUCE, OR PLAIN BUTTER.

Place it in a fish kettle with drainer in scalding water, a small piece of salt, and a good wine-glassful of vinegar (this is to preserve the colour) ; let it boil quickly up, then just bubble ; if the salmon is very thick, it will take nearly a quarter-of-an-hour to the pound ; a thin salmon trout will take from half-an-hour to three-quarters, according to its size, to cook it entirely ; when considered done, gently raise it up on the fish drainer ; if the head, fins, and tail, appear just breaking away, it is probably done, but the almost certain way to know is to take a thin wooden skewer, place it gently through the thick part, if it goes readily through it is done ; if it grizzles against the skewer it is not cooked enough ; this method may be tried without raising it. When ready, dish up on a fish drainer, and take care of the liquor in which it was boiled ; garnish with sprigs of fennel and parsley. Green peas are excellent with salmon. *The reason for setting salmon in scalding water with vinegar is, that it* SETS *the colour, and prevents the jelly of the fish from oozing out. For example : if any fish is placed in* COLD WATER, *and gently simmered for a few hours, the whole mass becomes a fish jelly. Sometimes fish is sent to table with the richness of the thin part—the most delicate —all turned to curd, occasioned by boiling fast ; the water must but scarcely be seen to bubble.*

ANCHOVY SAUCE.—Take half-a-pint of cold water, one table-spoonful of flour mixed smoothly, a very little salt ; strain, add two ounces of butter ; just simmer ; then put in one tablespoonful of Burgess's anchovy sauce, and one of Reading or Harvey sauce.

E

PICKLED SALMON.—Remove the bone, let the fish get cold; for a quart dish take half-a-pint of the fish liquor, a quarter of a teaspoonful of cayenne pepper, two or three broken-up bay-leaves, and a little fennel; boil it all with the liquor for half-an-hour, then strain to a pint of cold vinegar; mix well together, and pour over the fish; cover down closely; in two or three hours it may be eaten. This will keep well for more than a week in a cool place. If bay-leaves cannot be obtained, *six* allspice berries will do as well.

SALMON CUTLETS, DELICIOUS FOR LUNCHEON.—Have a cutlet of an inch-and-a-half in thickness cut off a nice thick salmon, butter a sheet of writing paper on one side, place the salmon on the buttered side, fold the paper well over, and turn it well over at the ends, so that no air can get in; put it in a tolerably hot oven on the oven plate; in fifteen minutes it will be ready; or put it on a gridiron over a very *clear slow fire.* The oven is best. When it is put in the oven, chop a tea-spoonful of capers fine, put to them a lump of butter the size of a small nut; when the cutlet is done, take off the paper, put into a very hot dish; on the top of the cutlet put the capers and butter, and a fringe of parsley or fennel all round.

BOILED MACKEREL.—April and May is the best time for this fish, when the fennel is springing; put them in hot water with a little salt, then simmer (not boil); they will be ready in a quarter-of-an-hour, and must be taken up the instant they are done; cover with sprigs of fennel and parsley; serve with *Fennel sauce.* Make this by throwing into boiling water with a little salt, a handful of fennel free from hard stems; after it boils reckon eight to ten minutes, according to its being old or young; then strain and chop finely; put it to melted butter; beat up well; or parsley and butter is excellent;

the parsley free from stem, thrown into boiling water, with a little salt ; after it boils, reckon two minutes ; chop finely, and put to melted butter ; one ounce of butter to a sauce-boat full.

PICKLED MACKEREL.—Place three clean unboiled mackerel in a quart pie dish, put on them some bay-leaves and a few all-spice berries, both bruised ; mix in a pint of vinegar, a quarter-of-a-teaspoonful of cayenne pepper, then pour on the fish ; cover with a flat dish on the top, and bake an hour and a half in a slow oven ; they will keep a week, or if any left boiled, pickle as for salmon, page 66.

FRIED WHITING—OR SMELTS—OR CRIMPED SKATE.

These should be cleaned, dried in a cloth, and dipped in batter, to make which, take three ounces, or three table-spoonfuls of flour, and a quarter-of-a-pint of milk ; mix it smoothly into a thick paste ; have ready a *very clean* frying-pan of *boiling* lard or bacon fat ; dip the fish in the batter, or place it on with a spoon, and place it instantly in the boiling fat ; an egg-slice is better to turn these with than a fish-slice ; do not turn them till they are quite brown on one side ; serve with plain melted butter, and sprigs of parsley around the dish.

SALT FISH—EGG SAUCE.

Buy that which has been already soaked, and which looks white and thick ; it must be purchased the day before, and soaked again in cold water for twelve hours, changing the water frequently ; put it in a fish kettle, with drainer, in cold water ; *never* let it boil ; *but after it just simmers* or the surface of the water just begins to move, reckon about twenty minutes, then lift the drainer to see if it is done ; the flakes of fish will then appear just falling apart ; some fish will take half-an-hour, or even more, according to its thickness. If it is not possible to

soak the fish the day before, well wash it in lukewarm water
several times, lay it in cold water, and when it comes to simmer,
throw the water away, and put it in fresh cold water; let it very
slowly simmer till it is done; serve with egg sauce, see page
68, and buttered parsnips, see page 27.

For Egg Sauce.—Put six eggs into cold water; let them
boil five minutes; when cold, peel, take the whites from the
yellow, and chop the whites fine; the yellows must be chopped
very little, and separately, or they will fall to powder. Take
three ounces of butter, half-a-pint of water, one tablespoonful of
flour; rub the flour and water into a smooth paste; put the
butter in; let it simmer (not boil); *no salt ;* then put in the
whites of the eggs, stir round, then put in the yellows, and just
beat up altogether with *a fork.*

Soles Fried in Batter—Anchovy Sauce.—Clean the
soles well by cutting them lower down than the fishmongers'
leave them; take out the blood which is inside; well wash and
wipe dry, flour and lay them in a cloth (if they have not been
skinned it is the black skin only which is taken off); prepare a
smooth batter of three tablespoonfuls of flour and a quarter of a pint of milk; dip the *skinned side* of the fish only in
this batter, put this skinned side downwards into a frying-pan,
that will hold two fish, half full of *boiling lard* or bacon
fat (some will use dripping, but it is not so well); when they
are of a nice golden brown colour, turn them by sticking a fork
in the head and a knife or fish slice under; when they are brown
both sides, they will be ready; take them up on to a hot dish
before the fire, to drain, not one on the other; and by the time
the second pair are done, the first will be drained, then lay the
first pair on a fish drainer or on the hot dish, in which they are to be
sent to table, and continue to do this till all are ready; serve

with plain melted butter, or with half a pint of picked shrimps in it, or with anchovy sauce (see page 65). The same lard can be used twice, if strained into water; the fat will float, the burnt bits sink.

SOLES FRIED WITH EGGS AND BREAD CRUMBS.—This method is really not so good as the batter, but causes more waste; rub sufficient bread crumbs through a colander into a broad dish; beat up one egg with a tablespoonful of milk; put this also into a broad dish; take the skinned side of the fish, dip this into the eggs, then into the bread crumbs, and place it in the boiling fat, this side downwards ; proceed to fry as directed in last receipt.

TO BOIL SOLES.—Take a frying pan that will hold either one fish or two, as may be wanted, *let it be very clean, fill it* with water and a little salt ; make *it simmer,* lay in the fish, the skinned side upwards but not one on the other; they must be covered with water, and will not require turning ; a quarter of an hour to twenty minutes will dress them; serve with plain melted butter, or with shrimps in the butter, which is best ; or parsley and butter.

TO BOIL TURBOT OR BRILL—LOBSTER SAUCE.—This fish is in season during most part of the summer, but best in the autumn ; two hours before cooking lay it in salt and cold water; when about to dress it, take up, wipe dry; cut it across the black thick skin of the back, lay this side downwards on the fish drainer in the kettle, in nearly scalding water, with a tablespoonful of salt; when it simmers, which it must very gently, reckon twenty minutes to half an hour according to thickness, for a piece of five or six pounds weight ; when ready (which can be told by lifting the drainer and examining ; if a whole fish, the fins, head, and tail will be cracking, if a small piece, the ends next the bone will be slightly raised from the bone); place it on a fish drainer the white side uppermost. Take the coral out of the head of the lobster, rub it through a small tin strainer, or coarse sieve, on to the top of the fish; garnish round with sprigs of parsley, and sliced lemon.

FOR LOBSTER SAUCE.—Spread the lobster on a table, with the tail straight; with a kitchen knife cut through from the head to the tail; avoid the stomach, which lies in a bag nearly on the point of the head; pick out the gut, which looks like a dark thread, frequently running from the head half way down the tail; pull the lobster in pieces with a fork in each hand; do not chop it; melt together two ounces of butter, half a pint of water, one tablespoonful of flour, first rubbed smoothly, free from lumps, then add one tablespoonful of anchovy sauce; when hot, put in the lobster, just cutting across the pieces that are too long; put in also all the pieces that are good, as well as the soft part from the head; when the lobster is put in the butter, give it one boil, then let all be dished as hot as possible.

DRIED HADDOCK; a breakfast dish.—Cut the two halves asunder; strike the skin side of each half two or three times on a table to loosen the skin; cut off the tail and strip the skin off upwards, lay the halves the bone side downwards, either on a gridiron, over a slow fire, or set them to toast before a quick, clear fire; let them be almost dressed on this side before turning, which should be in five minutes, then butter the side the skin was taken from, and brown up very quickly, then rub on a little more butter and slightly pepper with white pepper; serve very hot, with parsley round. Send the skinned side upwards to table.

To FRY SPRATS; better than broiled.—Wash them clean, let them drain in a cloth, and flour them; put a very tiny piece of butter in a frying pan, not much more than enough to grease it;

when very hot, throw in the sprats, they will quickly brown, then turn them, and when brown, send them up very hot indeed, well covered and with very hot plates; but very few should be sent up at a time; keep sending them hot and hot. Sprats, thus dressed will not disagree with those who eat them, the character of the oil they contain is changed.

To FRESHEN SHRIMPS THAT ARE DRY.——Pour on boiling water, let them remain in it five minutes, throw them into a colander, let the tap of cold water run on them till cold, shake them well in a cloth till dry; seven minutes is sufficient for the whole process.

To FRY FLOUNDERS AND PLAICE.——Wash clean and dry; then rub with salt, two hours before dressing; cook them as soles, (page 68); the plaice should have just the heads and tails cut off: then cut into two or three pieces according to the size.

EXCELLENT PUNCH TO BE DRUNK WITH FISH.——Make a lemonade of one wineglassful of lemon-juice, to eight wine-glassfuls of boiling water, and two wineglassfuls of loaf sugar, having previously rubbed the sugar slightly on the rind of lemon, when well mixed together and cold, strain and add two wine-glassfuls of brandy, and two of rum, then mix; this quantity will make about twelve wineglassfuls.

To SCALLOP OYSTERS.——See page 97.

PASTRY; PUDDINGS.

FOR PASTE FOR BAKED PIES, TARTS, &c., use as much again flour, as lard and butter together. For a quart pie dish sufficient for six or eight persons, take twelve ounces of flour, three ounces of lard, three ounces of butter; rub the lard well into flour; add a little water, sufficient to make into a paste, but scarcely touch it with the hand, use a spoon ; roll out lengthways ; spread half of the butter thinly over, slightly dredge a little flour over ; fold the paste over at the sides, then roll it up ; afterwards roll it out again the same way, being careful not to turn it ; spread the remainder of the butter over and slightly dredge flour ; then fold over the edges, and roll up ; now roll out to a size a little larger than will be wanted for the top of the dish ; place the dish upside down on it and cut the shape round ; with the remainder of the paste line the edges of the dish but not the bottom ; place in the fruit, and add sugar.

APPLE PIE.—To the sliced apples, put a few cloves and a little lemon-peel, then the sugar, put in a little ale or cider and cover the pie with the top, but make no hole in the middle of the paste ; crinkle the edges with the handle of a spoon ; let it bake an hour and a half.

RHUBARB PIE.—Wash well before cutting into pieces, do not skin unless very old ; take half a dozen stems in the hand at once and cut down through them with a sharp knife ; place in the dish ; add neither spice nor liquid, but from a quarter to half a pound of sugar ; take the same time as apple.

JAM OPEN TARTS.—Make the paste the same way ; cut it to the shape of the dish ; bake three quarters of a hour in a moderate oven ; take it out, put on the jam ; cover the top with open work of narrow strips of paste, or cut out forms with a pastry cutter ; return into the oven for a quarter of an hour. In this way the jam remains moist.

ROLLED JAM PUDDING.—Twelve ounces of flour, six of dripping, makes a pudding for six persons ; make the paste exactly as for a pie, only use dripping or lard ; after the second time rolling up, roll out into a long piece rather more than a quarter of a yard in width ; spread the jam rather thinly but evenly over the surface, then roll it up into as tight a roll as possible ; pinch it up at the ends ; place it in a wetted, well-floured pudding-cloth ; do not roll it in this, but fold in the edges of the cloth, so that it cannot burst through ; *pin* the cloth in two or three places in the length, tie up the ends ; put it in boiling water ; (a small fish-kettle is best with drainer at the bottom), make it boil up quickly, after it boils, reckon one hour.

GOOSEBERRY PIE.—Make the paste, as at page 71 ; the older the gooseberries the more sugar they take. A quart pie dish will take from a quarter of a pound to six ounces of sugar.

PLAIN SUET PUDDING.—Take twelve ounces of flour, six ounces of suet, which chop very fine ; rub this well into the flour with half a teaspoonful of salt, then add sufficient water to make into a stiff paste, roll it out thin, then roll it up, make it into a round ball, either tie it in a cloth, or in a well greased basin ; the latter makes it more shapely ; put into boiling water, after it boils reckon two hours.

DRIPPING PUDDING.—Twelve ounces of flour, six ounces of dripping, rub half the dripping into the flour with a little salt, mix with sufficient water to make into a stiff paste ; roll it out thin, put in the remainder of dripping, by spreading it thinly all over the paste, then roll it up in a roll, then roll it out thin, then roll it up again, and make into a round ball ; put it in a basin, tie down with a wetted well-floured cloth ; place in boiling water ; after it boils, reckon two hours. This makes an inexpensive light pudding for children, and eaten with jam or treacle, is excellent.

BAKED APPLE DUMPLINGS.—Make a paste as for either dripping or suet pudding, (page 71); after it is rolled out with rolling pin the last time, roll it up in a long roll, divide the paste into as many divisions as there are apples; pare, cut, and halve the apples; take out the core; stick two cloves in the place of core; roll slightly out one division of paste; place the two halves of apple together, and roll inside; well fasten up the joins of paste by rolling in the hand well floured; when all are made, place a bit of butter the size of a hazel-nut on the top of each dumpling; set in a baking tin, bake in a moderately warm oven, one hour to an hour and a half, according to the manner in which the oven will bake.

BOILED APPLE DUMPLINGS.—Make a paste, as at page 73 for dripping pudding, and proceed as for baked dumplings; only omit the butter; tie each up in a separate, wetted, well-floured cloth, throw into boiling water, make them quickly boil up; reckon one hour from this time.

APPLE FRITTERS, superior to those made with eggs.—Ingredients to serve four or six persons, costing 8½d. *Nine apples, eight ounces of flour, quarter of a pound of moist sugar, half a teaspoonful of allspice, pint of milk, three tablespoonfuls of ale; lard and lemon extra.* Pare and cut the apples into slices as large as possible without core, but not too thick; mix as much of the flour with the ale as will make into a thick smooth paste; let it stand an hour if there is time; take the remainder of flour, sugar, and spice, mix well together, then add part of the milk, and when ready to fry, mix the whole of the ingredients well, into a smooth batter; beat it well, throw in the apples; have a frying-pan very clean and half full of *boiling* lard, or dripping, but lard is nicer; stir up the batter and apples, drop some into the pan with a cup, letting two or three pieces of apple be in each fritter, which should be twice the size of the bowl of a table-spoon; when just set, add more till there are four or six, according to the size of pan ; fry of a light golden brown colour ; when done on both sides, set them on the fish-drainer, on a dish before the fire, to drain every drop of fat off; when this is done, send them to table on another hot clean dish, with moist sugar spread over, or white sugar sifted over, place a *strip* of lemon on each fritter; a lemon cut in halves should be on the table. *During the process of frying*, keep the pan clear of all little bits, which burn and discolour the lard ; recollect that no more lard or dripping is used by filling the pan half full, than by putting in little bits as it fries away, which is a very bad plan, as they require longer to dress, wastes more fat, and makes the food taste of the pan ; while the fritters look black instead of brown ; should there be any fat left in the pan after all are fried, throw it while boiling into a basin of cold water; the bits will sink to the bottom, the fat will float on the top when cold, and may be used for any other purpose again.

LEMON AND ORANGE FRITTERS.—Excellent as a winter dish when apples are scarce. Prepare the ingredients exactly as for apple fritters, only *mince* up very fine some candied orange or lemon peel, or put in some orange flavouring (page 86.)

SULTANA PUDDING, for six persons; to boil two hours.— Three quarters of a pound of Sultana raisins, 6d. ; eight ounces of flour, 1½d. ; four ounces of suet or dripping, 2d. ; quarter of a nutmeg, grated, ½d. ; three ounces of moist sugar, 1d. ; half a pint of milk, 1d. ; two eggs, 2d. ; total cost 1s. 2d. ; a basin to hold a pint and a half.—Wash the raisins well, pick them free from stems ; chop the suet fine, or if dripping, rub it well into the flour, rub in also the nutmeg and sugar : then add the raisins, and some orange shreds, see page 86; let the ingredients be equally mixed, then beat the eggs and milk together, mix with the flour, &c., and form it into a solid mass; rub a little dripping round a basin so that every part is greased; fill it with the dough, well working it with a spoon down to the bottom of the basin, which must be filled to the top; wet a pudding cloth and well flour it, tie securely over the top, pin up the corners of cloth over the basin to prevent slipping, plunge it in boiling water; after it boils reckon two hours.

A BOILED OR BAKED SWEET BATTER PUDDING.—*Six ounces of flour, two ounces of moist sugar, three eggs, whites and yolks, half a pint of milk, half a teaspoonful of nutmeg,* a pint basin; beat the milk, sugar, eggs and nutmeg together to a good froth till the sugar is dissolved, then strain and gradually mix this with the flour into a smooth batter of the thickness of cream; put it in a well buttered pint basin or one that will just hold it; tie a piece of writing paper over the top, then a wetted, well-floured cloth tied tightly over this; place it upside down in boiling water in a saucepan, not too large; after it boils up, reckon three hours. To bake, place it in a well buttered pie dish; bake it in a quick oven from an hour to an hour and a half; quick ovens will cause all batters to rise. For a quart basin use double quantity, and bake or boil as long again.

AN UNSWEETENED BATTER PUDDING.—Make exactly as above, using half a teaspoonful of salt instead of the sugar and nutmeg.

BAKED CUSTARD PUDDING.—This is made in five minutes and will serve six or eight persons. *Beat up one quart of milk, five eggs, whites and yolks, a quarter of a pound of moist sugar, half a teaspoonful of nutmeg; the expense of the whole will be*

9*d.* ; beat each egg separately and throw each into a jug ; put a little of the milk, then the sugar, and nutmeg, and beat up with the eggs ; then add the remainder of milk, and beat with a whisk into a froth ; pour into a quart dish ; bake an hour and a half, in a very slow oven ; if it is a hot oven, the milk will curdle and turn to whey, giving a watery appearance ; putting it in a cool oven at night will do.

BOILED RICE IN MILK, for six persons ; ready in one hour ; costing 10d.—*Ten ounces of rice, one quart of milk, quarter of a pound of moist sugar, half a nutmeg, two ounces of butter, a pint and a half of water.* Wash the rice quickly in warm water twice, put it in a clean tin saucepan with the water, cover close and shake it round occasionally ; in twenty minutes the rice should have taken up all the water ; then add the milk gradually, *allowing the cover to remain off* (this is to thicken the rice by allowing the steam to escape) ; when all the milk is in, add the butter, sugar, and nutmeg, stir it well together with a wooden spoon till it is a thick, rich mass ; be sure it does not burn ; when ready, turn it into a pie dish, then place a flat dish under.

LEMON CHEESECAKES.—*One pound of loaf sugar, six eggs, but the whites of four only, the juice of three large lemons, quarter pound of fresh butter ;* put these ingredients into a bright tin saucepan, over a slow fire, and stir very gently, till of the consistence of honey ; if to be used directly, make a paste of the proportion of six ounces of lard and six ounces of butter, to sixteen ounces of flour, and line the patty pans, then drop in sufficient of the mixture and bake from half an hour to three quarters ; otherwise, if not required for immediate use, tie down the mixture first with paper dipped in spirit, then securely over the top to keep out the air.

HASTY PUDDING, very excellent with sweet sauce.—This

pudding will cost 6d., and is enough for three or four persons. *Three eggs, whites and yolks, two piled tablespoonfuls of flour, two ounces of moist sugar, half a pint of milk, a little grated nutmeg ; a pint basin.* Dissolve the sugar in the milk, then beat the eggs, milk, and nutmeg well together, put the flour in a basin, add a little of the liquid to it, and rub the flour to a smooth batter ; then add the remainder of liquid, beat up well, put into the well-buttered basin, tie a piece of writing paper over the top, then a well-floured cloth tied tightly ; have ready a saucepan that will just hold it, of fast boiling water ; put it in with the cloth side downwards ; put a weight on the basin to keep it so till it boils, which it should do quickly, then reckon one hour.

FOR SWEET SAUCE, see page 80 ; raspberry vinegar poured over the above is delicious.

RICE PUDDING, for six persons.——Half a pound of rice, 1¼d., one pint of milk 2d., two eggs 2d., quarter of moist sugar 1d., one ounce of butter 1d., and nutmeg—7½d. ; one pint of cold water.——Wash the rice in warm water ; put it in a saucepan with a pint of cold water, let it stew very gently, when it has taken this up, turn it into a pan ; beat up the milk, eggs, sugar, and nutmeg, together, then well beat it up with the rice ; pour it into a pie dish, put the butter in small lumps on the top, grate nutmeg over ; bake one hour.

GROUND RICE PUDDING.——A quarter of a pound of ground rice, a pint and a half of milk, mixed smoothly together ; set it on the fire, keeping it well stirred ; *it will quickly burn* if left ; when well simmered to a good thick batter, put in an ounce of butter, three ounces of sugar, and a little nutmeg, beat up well together, and when nearly cold, add three well beaten eggs, with whites, strain these to the pudding, and well beat up together ; turn it into a quart pie dish, place little bits of butter all over the top, and a little more nutmeg; bake three quarters of an hour; or put into a well buttered basin with paper over the top, and a well floured cloth tied tightly over that, place it in fast boiling water; after it boils up reckon an hour.

A BOILED OR BAKED BREAD PUDDING—*To be prepared over night.*—One pound of bread 2d., two ounces of butter 1½d., quarter of a pound of moist sugar 1d., half a teaspoonful of nutmeg ¼d., half a pint of milk 1d., two eggs 1½d., quarter of a pound of sultana raisins, 2½d. (or a pound of fresh plums, damsons, or cherries), total, 10d.; one pint boiling water; quart basin.—Over night, break the bread into small pieces in a pan, pour the boiling water on the sugar, butter, and nutmeg; beat up well together, then pour it on the bread, covering every part; the next day, beat the eggs and milk together, then add to the bread and beat with a wooden spoon into a hard, smooth mass; mix up well with it the raisins or fruit; butter the basin, fill it very full, tie it down with a wetted, well-floured cloth; put the pudding upside down in boiling water; make it boil quickly; afterwards reckon two hours to boil; two and a half hours to bake, which latter may be in a basin, but must not be tied down.

A QUICKLY-MADE BREAD PUDDING.—Half a pound of bread crumbs, one pint of milk, three ounces of moist sugar, half a teaspoonful of nutmeg, a little orange or lemon flavouring, if liked, (see page 86), three eggs. Rub some stale bread through a colander into a large basin, then mix in some orange or lemon flavouring; make the milk boil; pour over the bread; put a plate on the top of the basin to keep in the steam; beat the eggs up in a jug with a tablespoonful of water; add the sugar and nutmeg; beat up together, then stir into the bread; mix up well, and fill a well-buttered basin quite full; tie down with writing paper, then over that a wetted, well-floured cloth; place upside down in a saucepan of boiling water; after it boils up, reckon one hour.

BREAD AND BUTTER PUDDING, for six or eight persons.—Four eggs 3d., quart of milk 4d., quarter of a pound of sugar 1d., bread and butter and nutmeg 2d., orange flavouring. Total 10d. Cut some thin small slices of bread and butter (free from crust if preferred, spread the butter very thin), place a layer in the bottom of a good sized quart pie dish; sprinkle over a few orange shreds (see page 86), add another layer of bread and butter with more orange, then a layer *without* orange; break each egg separately into a cup (to prevent a bad one spoiling the whole) throw each after it is broken into a jug, now beat up eggs and whites, milk, sugar, and nutmeg into a froth till the sugar is dissolved, pour through a tin strainer on to the bread and butter; bake in a cool oven two hours, if the oven is hot it will turn the milk to *whey*, or watery; *this* is always the fault of *too hot an oven*, not of the milk.

SWEET WHITE SAUCE FOR BREAD PUDDING.—One ounce of butter, one ounce of flour, two teaspoonfuls of white sugar, half a pint of milk. Mix the flour and milk gradually together so that it is not lumpy: add the sugar and butter, melt together, shaking it one way till it is a little thick, then strain. Brandy or wine sauce is made the same, using water. Cream is made as white sauce, only leaving out the flour, and instead, beating up the yolk of an egg with the milk, setting it in a cup or basin in a saucepan of boiling water, on the fire till it thickens.

BAKED TAPIOCA PUDDING.—Six ounces Tapioca, three ounces moist sugar, one ounce of butter, one pint of milk, one pint of cold water, two eggs, half a teaspoonful of nutmeg, a little orange flavouring, if liked, (page 86); a quart pie dish. Wash the Tapioca well, in slightly warm water, changing it three times *(this will take off the earthy taste)*; put it in a saucepan, over a slow fire, with one pint of water and half a pint of milk; let it thicken, keeping it frequently stirred till the tapioca rises to the top and remains there, or till the tapioca has soaked up all the liquid; then turn it into the dish, stir it well and let it remain till half cold; then mix in the orange flavouring, or any other which is liked; beat up the eggs, sugar, and nutmeg, and remainder of milk, to a good froth, or till the sugar is dissolved; then strain this to the tapioca and well beat up with a wooden spoon till the eggs and milk are thoroughly mixed; then place the butter, cut up into small bits, over the top, to prevent the top from burning; bake in a moderate oven, till set quite thick and of a bright brown colour; the time will vary from an hour, to an hour and a half, according to the oven. *To save time in making this and sago pudding and also to prevent waste, put the sago or tapioca into the quart dish with the milk and water; place it in the oven for an hour or so, keeping it stirred occasionally, also beat it up well with a wooden spoon now and then, and when sufficiently thick, proceed as directed.*

SAGO PUDDING, exactly as above.

CHRISTMAS PUDDING.—Ingredients: *two pounds of stale bread crumbs, quarter of a pound of flour, one pound of currants, one pound of stoned and chopped raisins, one and a half pound of suet finely chopped, half a pound of candied peel, one pound of moist sugar, half an ounce of mixed spice, and eight eggs;* this will cost about 4s. 5d., but is very delicious; it is best boiled in two quart basins; rub the bread through a colander; well wash the raisins *before stoning;* clean, pick, and wash the cur-

F

rants ; rub the flour, bread, spice, and sugar together first, then add the suet, chop the raisins, then mix them, then the currants ; cut the candied peel into thick lumps, and well mix ; when everything is thoroughly blended together beat up the eggs, and *strain* into the pudding ; it now requires well mixing with a wooden spoon ; butter and fill the basin ; be careful to force the pudding down into and round the basin ; fill quite to the top ; tie up in a wetted, well-floured cloth : put into fast boiling water, which must again boil quickly up ; then reckon six hours ; the pudding is best made the day before it is wanted ; do not take it out of the basin, but put it to rewarm in the oven for an hour, or it may be tied in a cloth and boiled one hour, putting it in boiling water.

PLUM-PUDDING SAUCE.—One teaspoonful of flour rubbed into a smooth batter, with a quarter of a pint of water, two ounces of butter melted with it, then add a wineglassful of sherry or brandy.

A BAKED BATTER PUDDING, with Sultanas and Apples, or Sultanas alone.—Quarter of a pound of sultanas 2d., half-a pound of flour 2½d., quarter of a pound of sugar 1d, a little nutmeg, a pint of milk 2d., two eggs 1½d., three or four sliced apples. Cost 10d. ; oval tin, twelve inches long and eight inches wide ; beat the eggs, sugar, nutmeg, and milk together ; mix them gradually with the flour, till it is a smooth paste or batter, free from lumps ; wash and pick the sultanas, pare, and slice the apples without core, warm the tin, grease it well with beef dripping or butter, the dripping is equally good ; place a layer of sultanas over the bottom of the tin, then beat up the batter, well strain into the tin, put some small lumps of dripping on the top, bake in a moderate oven for an hour and a quarter ; then, without taking out of the oven, place a layer of apples over the top, bake another half hour, then put a hot dish on the top of the baking tin, turn the pudding over with it, thus the side with the sultanas will be uppermost; sift a little crystalized or white sugar over it, and send up hot.

CHRISTMAS CAKE FOR A PARTY.—Take one pound of flour, one pound of sifted white sugar, the rind of a lemon grated, half a teaspoonful of nutmeg; mix well together; take eight eggs (NOTE— *All eggs must be used with their whites, unless otherwise directed)* beat into a froth, and strain; mix by degrees with the other ingredients; beat well with a wooden spoon in a pan for a full hour, *without ceasing;* bake in a buttered tin in a quick oven for two hours, *allowing it to cool gradually,* that is, it must be put on the oven or near the fire when taken out, and loosened from the tin, by setting the cake up edgeways on the tin.   Many persons prefer to buy a cake from the confectioners; it is less trouble, and certain to be good; whereas cakes depend so much on the beating and baking that they frequently turn out failures.   To buy a good-sized sponge cake will cost 2s. 6d.; it should be made *two days* before it is wanted; the day before it is to be used, place it in a deep glass dish, a china bowl, a salad bowl, or even a deep vegetable dish will do; mix three wineglassfuls of sherry and one of brandy together; pour this over the cake; add more if not thoroughly soaked; cover with a large basin till next day; now make a *Boiled Custard* thus :—Take three pints of milk, a little lemon-peel, a little nutmeg or powdered cinnamon, quarter of a pound of loaf sugar, two bay leaves, half a dozen peach leaves, or three bitter almonds, or one laurel leaf bruised; *put on cold,* and boil for ten minutes; mix smoothly in a basin a piled tablespoonful of arrowroot, with a little cold milk; beat separately the yolks of six eggs; mix with the arrow root and milk; then strain the boiling-hot milk to this cold, which must be done gradually, and beating the cold eggs and milk all the time ; set it to thicken on the fire (*if it boils, or even simmers, it will curdle ; a good plan is to pour it into a jug, and stand the jug in a sauce-pan of fast boiling water, stirring or shaking the custard round one way till sufficiently thick*) ; then put in a bowl two table-spoonfuls of brandy ; pour the custard on it, and stir well till cold ; if suffered to stand instead of being stirred, a head will form on the top, and the custard will be lumpy ; when cold pour the custard round the cake ; blanch some almonds by pouring boiling water on them ; the skins will then peel off ; cut the almonds in strips, and stick over the cake.   In helping, be careful to cut the cake out with a spoon ; help some custard round it, not on it.

MINCE PIES.—Ingredients, one pound of flour, six ounces of lard, six ounces of butter ; make this into paste as directed, (page 71), but use the above quantities.   One pound of undercut of sirloin of beef, two ounces of suet, six apples, half-an-ounce of mixed spice, two ounces of candied peel, half-a-pound of stoned and finely-chopped raisins, half-a-pound of currants, quarter-of-a-pound of moist sugar ; line the tins ; cut the covers of paste ; mince the beef and suet very finely together, put it in a dish in the oven for half-an-hour, then take up and beat well together till cold ; chop the raisins, clean and pick the currants, cut the peel in *thin* slices, which cut across again, peel and chop the apples very fine ; mix all separately, even the sugar and spice, into the beef; fill the tins, cover them ; bake from half to three-quarters-of-an-hour, in a moderate oven, when done and taken out, gently lift each cover of paste and put in one teaspoonful of brandy.   These are very rich eating.   They may be made plainer by omitting the beef, putting an extra half-pound of both currants and raisins, the latter well chopped.

PLAIN PLUM PUDDING.—For sauce, see page 82; one pound of flour, half-a-pound of currants, half-a-pound of Sultana raisins, half a grated nutmeg, half-a-pound of moist sugar, one pound of suet, half-a-pint of milk; chop the suet very fine, mix with the spice, sugar, and flour together; wash and pick the raisins and currants, mix well, then add the milk till made into a stiff paste; boil in a wetted well-floured cloth three hours, or bake the same time.

TEA CAKES.—Rub a quarter-of-a-pound of fresh butter into three-and-a-half pounds of flour, make a hole in the centre; mix together a teacupful of yeast, and the same of warm milk; set this in the middle of the flour; cover it with a thick cloth or flannel; let it stand an hour in a warm place; make it up into a light dough, with as much *nearly* cold milk as it requires; work it well with the hands; divide the quantity into eight cakes; bake in buttered tins in an oven more than moderately warm, half-an-hour. If baked on a dish, three-quarters-of-an-hour.

TEA CAKE FROM BAKERS' DOUGH.—Take a half-quartern of dough, one pound of dripping, quarter-of-an-ounce of allspice, two ounces of candied peel chopped fine, or a little orange flavouring (page 86); roll out the dough as thin as possible, place in half the dripping, exactly as in making pastry, also half the peel; fold it up, then roll it out again; put in remainder of dripping and peel, fold it up, roll out again, then roll up into form; bake in a buttered tin two hours, in a moderately warm oven; in taking it out of the tin, when baked, turn it upside down on the edge of the tin, but not take it directly into a cold place.

SWEET CAKES FROM PASTRY DOUGH.—When any is left, roll it out very thin, sift some sugar and a little ginger over it, fold it up, roll out again, then roll up and divide into cakes ; bake on a dish.

AN EXCELLENT CAKE, HOT OR COLD.—Take one pound of bakers' dough, roll out thin, spread in at twice rolling out, half-a-pound of lard, sprinkle a little salt the first time ; make it up into a flat cake, about half-a-finger deep ; bake on a tin or dish an hour-and-a-half.

EXCELLENT LITTLE CAKES.—Mix a quarter-of-a-pound of well-dried flour, with a quarter-of-a-pound of sifted loaf sugar, and a quarter-of-a-pound of well washed and dried currants ; a quarter-of-a-pound of fresh butter, melted before the fire, beat all up together, then add the yolk and white of one egg beaten together and strained ; now beat up the whole for ten minutes, then roll out, divide into twenty-four pieces, make into round cakes ; bake on a tin twenty minutes ; if baked on a dish, they will take longer.

SCOTCH SHORT BREAD.—One pound of flour well dried, ten ounces of sifted loaf sugar, three-quarters-of-a-pound of butter slightly melted, ten drops of essence of almonds ; mix and add sufficient milk to make into a stiff paste, then roll out an inch thick ; bake in a tin three-quarters-of-an-hour.

ORANGE AND LEMON FLAVOURING.—Before giving oranges to children, pare the yellow rind off very thin ; *there must be none of the white;* also the same from lemons, only keep them separate ; cut these rinds into narrow shreds ; put them in a clean pickle bottle, or any other with a wide mouth, and which a broad cork will fit ; put layers of rind and layers of crys-talized moist sugar ; when the bottle is full, pour in a little (say two tablespoonfuls) of home-made wine, or brandy, or gin ; in a week it may be used, and it may be constantly added to, and will quite supersede the candied peel; it is used for flavouring bread and butter pudding, as well as those made from flour.

BLANC MANGE.—As Blanc Mange is a luxury which should be made very good, it is useless to offer a cheap substitute. The quantities given will fill two small moulds or one large one. The cost will be 3s. :—Pint and a half of milk, 3d. ; half a pint of cream, 1s. 3d. ; quarter of a pound of loaf sugar, 2d. ; one and quarter ounce of isinglass, 1s. 3d. ; almonds, spice, and lemon-peel, 1d. In the milk, boil for half an hour six bitter almonds, a small stick of cinnamon, a little lemon-peel, and the sugar ; then *strain* to the isinglass, and boil this till the latter is dissolved ; then strain to the cream in a jug, beat it together well, let it stand an hour, wet the moulds in cold water, pour the mixture very gently into these, so that the sediment remains in the jug ; then put by in a cool place till next day. To turn out of the moulds, run the finger round between the mould and blanc mange, just at the edge, and turn upside down on the dish in which it is to be served.

VEGETABLES.

TO BOIL POTATOES.—These must first be washed then pared ; take out all the eyes, and throw them into a pan of clean water ; if old potatoes, put on in cold water, barely just enough to cover them, with a little salt ; if young, in boiling water, with a little salt ; to steam they will take an hour ; this latter is almost a certain way of cooking well all kinds, excepting very young potatoes ; they should only be cooked the

minute before they are to be served, and well drained, and that
minute they should be put in a dish in the oven to dry; never
put a cover on, or the steam goes back into the potatoes.

To Fry Potatoes for Breakfast or Supper.—No meat or
bacon is required to be eaten with these; in Somersetshire it
forms the only breakfast dish of the peasantry, many of the
middle classes, and is frequently seen at the tables of the
wealthy, throughout the year. If potatoes are left from dinner,
these will do; if not, boil some the day before frying, but if over-
boiled they will not be good; *when cold*, chop them very fine,
as fine as for suet, *but not mash them*: sprinkle a little salt over;
for a vegetable-dish full of potatoes, have in a frying-pan about
two tablespoonfuls of dripping or bacon-fat, *made boiling hot;*
put in the potatoes, stir them about well; when hot through,
put them together with the knife or spoon (but not press them)
into about the size of the dish they are to be served on; now
let them brown for ten minutes; then, when brown, place the dish
on the top, and turn them over; serve them hot, with hot plates.

French Fried Potatoes.—Cut new potatoes in thin slices,
put them in boiling fat, and a little salt; fry both sides of a
light golden brown colour; drain dry from fat, and serve hot.

Broad Beans.—Must be put in boiling water, with a little
salt; boil fast for twenty minutes or half an hour; serve with
parsley and butter.

Boiled Rice as a Vegetable.—Take half a pint of rice,
well wash twice in warm water, pick out discoloured grains,
throw the rice into a quart of cold water, make it quickly boil;
then reckon twenty minutes; it should have taken up all the
water, or it has not been kept fast boiling; should any water be
left, drain it off; the rice will be quite white, and each grain
separate.

To Boil Artichokes.—First wash them very clean in warm water; then peel all over; put them in cold water as they are peeled; pick out all eyes and specks; don't keep them out of water a minute; boil them in a saucepan of boiling water, with a little salt; in half an hour they should be ready, but they must boil up quickly, and keep so; when done, drain them very dry (if they are to be used directly; if not, keep them in the water, or they will turn black; this and sea-kale are the only vegetables that can be allowed to stand in the water a few minutes); then mash them with a bit of dripping the size of a walnut, and a little pepper; serve them very hot, and well drained.

Harico Beans to Boil, also in Gravy.—Half a pint of beans will make a large dish full; wash them, and put on in a good-sized saucepan, in cold water, *but that the water cannot be seen above them;* set over a *very* slow fire, and stew gently for two hours, adding a very little water as the beans become dry. They will be perfectly soft if attended to, but if sufficient water to *cover them* is put at first they will never dress properly. When done, strain; then make gravy thus:—In a frying-pan put a table-spoonful of dripping, when boiling mix in a piled tea-spoonful of flour, and a little salt, let the dripping slightly brown; then add a quarter of a pint of hot water by degrees, and a table-spoonful of browning; when thick enough put the gravy to the beans, and serve very hot, or serve with plain melted butter, though it is not nearly so good.

• *For other Vegetables look to* Index.

To Roast Apples.—*Roll them tightly in paper,* to shut out all air; then put them in an oven, or on the hob; keep turning them till done.

To PICKLE CABBAGE.—Choose one of a dark copper colour, and pointed in shape; pick off the outside leaves; wipe it dry; cut the cabbage in thin slices; put it in a pan, with a layer of salt and layer of cabbage alternately; let it stand twenty-four hours; drain, and spread about in a large broad dish; then pour *boiling* water *over the whole;* let it stand two minutes; then drain, and remain till quite cold; fill the jars; pour cold spiced vinegar upon it; tie it down; in three days it will be fit for eating; the jars should be small; the cabbage should only be touched with a wooden spoon.

SPICED VINEGAR FOR CABBAGE.—Take half a pint of vinegar, put in a teaspoonful of cayenne, a dozen cloves, a dozen allspice berries, a piece or two of ginger; let it boil half an hour; then strain to the remainder of vinegar; let it get cold, and pour on the cabbage.

To PICKLE ONIONS.—Get a quart of silver onions, throw them unpeeled into a saucepan of boiling water; let them boil up once; drain, and they will easily peel, if done quickly; throw them into a cloth on dish, spread open, that they may cool quickly; fill the jars, and pour over them spiced vinegar, as for cabbage, only omitting the cayenne; they will not be white, but wholesome and relishing

-----

PRESERVES.

RED CURRANT JELLY.—Boil three pints of currants, free from stalks, strain; this will give about a pint of juice. To this add a pound of loaf sugar, or as much more in the same proportion as there may be juice. Simmer slowly for half an hour, or till the juice will set. Try this by dropping a little on a cold plate; it should be firm if sufficiently boiled. Be careful to scum well. When done, pour into very small jars till cold, then put papers soaked in gin, then tie down securely.

CHERRIES IN GIN.—Take Morella cherries, when black ripe, run a fine needle through each cherry, put them into a wide-mouth bottle, a pickle bottle will do, with layers of powdered loaf sugar and layers of cherries, with a few cloves, let them stay a night; add more cherries and sugar if the others have sunk, then fill up with gin, then cork them down. They will be ready in two months, and in the winter is an agreeable and cheap substitute for wine.

JAMS—RHUBARB, BLACK CURRANT, RASPBERRY, GOOSEBERRY, may be made with three quarters of a pound of moist sugar to a pound of fruit, boiled for about half an hour in a tin saucepan, stirred with a wooden spoon. They should be simmered till no scum arises, then poured into jars. Tie down next day first with paper soaked in gin, then tie down tight with other paper, and keep in a place neither too dry nor damp.

STRAWBERRY JAM.—Take a pint of red currant juice, simmer a pound and a half of loaf sugar with this for ten minutes; then put in a pound of strawberries, and simmer for half an hour. This is delicious, preserving the delicate taste of the fruit, with an agreeable acidity.

DAMSON JAM.—Three quarters of a pound of *crystalized* sugar (not loaf or pounded loaf) to each pint or pound of damsons. Two quarts, or four pints of damsons, will make four jars, each containing nearly a pound of jam.

Put the damsons and sugar into a new tin saucepan, and boil from half to three quarters of an hour over a very slow fire; scum well. When sufficiently done, take out all the stones and crack, mix the kernels with the jam, turn out the jam into the jars to cool; after three days cover the jam with paper soaked in gin, then with other paper securely tied over the jar. Keep in a cool, dry place. In two months examine, and if signs of "boiling," or fermenting, boil down again, and place fresh gin papers on the top; afterwards tie down securely.

EXCELLENT JAM may be made every week, from any fruit, by boiling a pound of fruit to half a pound of moist sugar for half an hour. Most children will prefer this to butter; but it will not keep longer than a week.

RHUBARB WINE, *most excellent if made according to directions.*— Ingredients for one gallon: six pounds of rhubarb stalks, one gallon of water, four pounds of loaf sugar, one lemon, a quarter of an ounce of isinglass (not gelatine).

In September, when the rhubarb is woody, bruise, with a wooden mallet in a tub, six pounds of stalks to a mash; pour on this one gallon of hard water, let it lie six days, stirring it up three times a day; on the sixth day strain it through a coarse sieve, then again through a sieve of doubled muslin; now add four pounds of powdered loaf sugar, and one lemon, sliced very thin; let this be stirred till the sugar is dissolved; not stir it afterwards, but let it stand in this state ten days. Then, without disturbing the dregs, strain it off through doubled muslin; then place it in a two-gallon jar, uncorked, in a cellar where no insect can creep into it. At the end of eight or ten weeks fermentation will have ceased; then put into it the isinglass, dissolved in a table-spoonful of boiling water; then cork it down. In six months pour it very gently out of the jar, and bottle it, first placing a lump of sugar in each bottle; cork with new corks, and tie down securely. In twelve months it is equal to any foreign light wine.

SICK-ROOM DIET.

To make Beef Tea for very weak Invalids.—Take three pounds of very lean beef, cut off every particle of fat—not use this. Cut the beef in thick slices, score it well across on both sides, put to it a pint and a half of cold water, simmer it slowly till it is reduced to half a pint ; pour this off, put it in a cool place, add another pint and half, serve this the same ; and again another pint and half, until there is a pint and half of thick animal jelly. When cold take off the fat, warm up the tea, add a little salt, pour it into a bottle, cork it tight. If when cold it will not freely come out, place the bottle in warm water.

For Ordinary Beef Tea.—A pound of meat will make a pint of tea ; therefore to a pound of meat must be put a quart of water ; simmer till reduced to a pint. If there is much weakness in the patient it should be given cold.

To make Mutton Broth.—Boil a pound of scrag of mutton in a quart of water till reduced to a pint, add a little salt and a little colouring or burnt sugar (see page 24), then strain. When cold, take off the fat, re-warm the broth, and pour over little squares of well-toasted bread.

To make Arrow-Root.—Make boiling a pint of milk ; rub smoothly, in a basin, a dessert-spoonful of arrow-root, the same of sugar, and a little nutmeg, with as small a quantity of cold milk as is sufficient ; pour the boiling milk on this, keep stirring till it thickens. A glass of sherry, or port wine, may be poured to this if liked ; but it must be beaten up quickly, or it will curdle.

For Pudding, add an egg to this, and bake it.

GRUEL should be made from Robinson's Patent Groats, and made according to directions given on the paper.

BARLEY WATER; *a delicious Drink for Coughs, Fevers, and great Thirst.*—Take the Prepared Barley, sold by all grocers and chemists, rub a dessert-spoonful of it in a little cold water till smooth, pour on this a quart of boiling water and two ounces of loaf sugar, let it boil twenty minutes, very slowly, or it will boil over. Then squeeze a lemon into it, strain, and pour backwards and forwards till cold, then bottle.

TO MAKE TOAST AND WATER.—Bake a thick small piece of bread, not crust, till it is of a deep brown, not black; pour over it a quart of boiling water, wrap a wet cloth round the jug, but not over it, which will rapidly cool it; put in a cool place.

BREAD AND MILK FOR AN INVALID.—Cut up a round of bread, free from crust if not liked, into square pieces, put it into a pint of milk, with a lump of butter the size of a hazel nut; and sugar if liked; let it boil, stirring it frequently; ten minutes will cook it.

DRY TOAST.—Cut the bread off the bottom part of the loaf, that is, cutting the entire under crust off; toast it at first at some distance from the fire to let the steam escape, then put it gradually nearer till it becomes of a light golden brown; then turn it, toast the other side the same, set it upright with a fork, or put it in a toast-rack, or it will eat tough. If there are many rounds to bake, set the rack, with that which is toasted before the fire. Buttered toast should be made free from toughness. Where there is an oven spread the bread on a dish, and put it in for a few minutes to allow the steam to dry.

SUNDRIES.

To MAKE SAUSAGES WITHOUT SKIN.——Chop very finely any cold or raw meat with a little of the fat ; add one-third of sifted bread crumbs ; mix separately equal portions of salt, pepper, and dried sifted sage, with a little ground allspice ; mix this with the meat.   Obtain a funnel, with the end, or pipe, nearly as large round as an egg-cup, and of a finger's length (*a funnel can be made of this size for one shilling, and is very useful for filling tea or coffee canisters*) ; dip this end in flour, also flour a plate ; push the meat very hard through the funnel on to the plate ; roll the rolls of meat well in flour (*all this should be prepared the day before wanted*).   Have ready a small frying-pan of *boiling* dripping or lard ; beat up an egg white and yolk, with a spoon baste the rolls with the egg ; take them up with an egg-slice, place them in boiling fat, and well brown ; drain them dry from fat ; have ready some toast, either dry or buttered on one side ; cut to the size of the sausages, serve them on this with sprigs of parsley round.

TOASTED CHEESE.——Have ready a gridiron, on a clear, slow fire ; put some bits of butter on a flat dish, with two table-spoonfuls of beer or ale ; cut some thin slices of cheese into this dish till an inch thick, spread thinly some mustard over, and a little pepper ; put the dish on the gridiron ; in ten minutes it will be ready. Have a hot buttered toast ready in a very hot dish, slip the cheese on to this, and cut into large squares—serve very hot.   Or if toast is not liked, send it up on the same dish in which it is cooked, merely placing this dish on another a little larger ; if more is required, take another dish.   Or have ready a crisp toast, buttered on both sides ; cut some very thin slices of cheese on this, or grate some ; spread a very little mustard over, then toast quickly before the fire ; cut through into sizeable pieces—send to table very hot.

To MAKE TEA.—For one person, a tea-spoonful, put into a brown-ware tea-pot, wetted half an hour before wanted, and placed in the oven, will make better tea than three spoonfuls in the ordinary way.

To MAKE TEA FOR A FAMILY.—Pour boiling water in the tea-pot, *then put the tea in ;* in five minutes it will sink to the bottom. Better tea will be made with three spoonfuls of tea than with five ordinarily. The old rule of one teaspoonful for each person and one for the tea-pot is a good one.

COFFEE.—It is best to buy a pound of coffee in berry, at 1s. 4d., and half a pound of chicory, at 3d. Mix them together in a dish, put it on or in a cool oven for two or three hours, then grind. Thus a pound and a half costs 1s. 7d. A tablespoonful of coffee, or two piled teaspsoonfuls for each person, made in one of Gilbert's coffee-pots, will make three quarters of a pint of excellent coffee, such as the French use. Use boiled milk, in the proportion of one-third to the cup.

To MAKE MUSTARD.—Take the proportions of one teaspoonful of mustard and half a teaspoonful of salt, mix to a smooth paste with cold water ; beat up for five minutes. The salt preserves the mustard, and the beating makes it thoroughly mix—*there must be no lumps.*

TABLE SALT.—Dry two lumps of salt, grate one against the other into a hair sieve, then sift. To divide large pieces of salt, take a kitchen knife, and hammer or poker, place the knife across as if to divide, hammer the knife into the salt, it will then fall into pieces.

To Recover Tainted Meat.—Meat or poultry, that has been suddenly turned with the weather, may be easily made sweet by having a saucepan of boiling water ready, in which put a small piece of charcoal, then put in the meat for ten minutes. If charcoal is not kept in the house, it is easily made by taking a reel which has held cotton, putting it in the middle of a clear fire, near the bar of the grate, till it is quite red ; take it out instantly it looks like this, and plunge it into cold water. Deal wood will not do, nor any wood which has turpentine in it.

To Scallop Oysters.—Take off the beards or *black frill*, set them in a dish or tin ; rub some bread crumbs through a colander over them, sprinkle a little salt and pepper and a tiny bit of butter on each oyster ; set the dish slanting before a clear fire for ten minutes till they are brown ; when done place the dish or tin on another dish with sprigs of parsley on the top of the oysters, or round the outer dish to hide the tin.

USEFUL SUNDRIES.

To Clean Lamp Glasses that are Smoked.—After washing them in warm water, soap, and soda, pour some vitriol into the water ; let them remain in it a short time, then rinse in clean water, and wipe dry. The end of a skewer will push the flannel and cloth through the tube of glass. After washing lay the glass before the fire till gradually cool ; and when any glass has to be screwed on, screw it on warm. The meaning of this is, that glass stretches with heat and shrinks with cold ; so that if heat is suddenly applied they snap, or after they have been in warm water or vitriol ; the sudden chill of the air causes them also to snap directly

G

the lamp is lighted.   In frosty weather always hold them to the fire before lighting the lamp.

To CLEAN PLATE AND PLATED DISH COVERS.—Wash well in very hot water, soap, and soda ; clean out all corners with a brush (a nail-brush is best that has bristles at the end).   As each article is washed, place it in a pan of clear almost boiling water—this will take out all the soap.   Then wipe dry, take a clean Chamois leather, rub some dry whitening on the leather, then rub the plate.   If any tarnish remains, wet a little whiting, rub it on well, then rub off.   Wash the leather in soap, soda, and slightly warm water every week, not dry it by the fire, and rub well while drying to render it soft.   One leather should last a twelvemonth with ordinary care, and may then be taken for scouring leather.

To CLEAN TIN OR BRITANNIA METAL DISH-COVERS, TEA AND COFFEE POTS, SPOONS, &c.—Wash the articles well in warm water and soda, with a piece of flannel, rub out the dirt in the crevices with a brush, wipe dry, then take a damp piece of rag, dip it in some crocus (a pennyworth obtained at an oilshop, will last a month), rub this very hard over the tins, let it slightly dry, then rub off with washleather dipped in dry crocus, and rub the crocus out of the crevices with a brush like a tooth-brush ; then rub well all over with plain washleather.   The crocus should be kept in a box.

To CLEAN FURNITURE.—Clean off all old stains and dirt with cold tea ; let it be quite dry, take a hard piece of bee's-wax, hold it in the warm hand till a little soft, rub on a sixpenny hard shoe-brush quite new (it must be kept for this purpose), a little wax, then rub the furniture, polish with a chamois leather.   This polish is hard, will not mark, is readily applied, and will last longer than any. The leather need not be washed more than once in two months.

Or there is a polish sold called "Lux Liquida," which is very excellent.

To CLEAN COMMON BRIGHT STOVES.—Rub two pieces of Flanders brick one against the other; the fine dust which falls is excellent, either mixed with water to rub off rust, or dry to polish with, or with a very little oil. When black-leaded stoves will not polish well, cover with a coat of STREETS' Brunswick black; to be had at any oil-shop; a shilling jar will cover three or four stoves. It must have dried for a week before black-leading.

For the best polished steel stoves use a mixture of the finest Tripoli powder and a little crocus; for brass work crocus only.

To CLEAN BURNED DISHES, AND TARNISHED EGG OR TEA-SPOONS.—Wet the article, rub on dry salt.

To TAKE OUT FRESH INK STAINS.—Immediately put the stain in milk, which change frequently.

HINTS FOR COMFORT AND CLEANLINESS.

To MAKE FLOORS LOOK WHITE, AND PURIFY A ROOM AT THE SAME TIME.—Take a pound of chloride of lime, mix it in a pail of cold water, stir it up well, then with an old broom apply it all over the boards; let it remain some hours, or till next day, then with clean water scrub them well. *Never scrub rooms with soap, it gets into the crevices of the boards, and cannot be got out.*

To SCRUB ROOMS.—Never scrub rooms with soap, the grease gets into the roughness of the boards; they always look dirty

Use soda and hot water, with a cocoa-nut fibre brush; scrub the way of the grain of the boards. *In cleaning paint, rub the way of the brush marks in the paint; use a very little soda, no soap, and wipe very dry each pannel at a time.*

FOR CHAPPED HANDS.—Cut off a piece of lemon and rub in, or wash the hands in vinegar: This is a sure remedy, and only sharp at first.

FOR CHILBLAINS.—Soak the hands or feet in very hot water for ten minutes, but it must be *very hot;* then rub them hard with spirits of turpentine; roll both hands and feet in stockings to keep out the air; doing this three nights following will cure the worst chilblains, and possibly they will not return for years; the turpentine must not be used with *broken* chilblains, but may be where they are only in a bladder; keep the turpentine from fire and candle, or great harm will arise.

SURE REMEDY TO DESTROY BUGS.—Put in a pail seven pounds of salt, fill it three parts full of boiling water; when it is quite dissolved, if it will take more salt, add more; it must be a strong and somewhat clear brine; with a brush apply this to the crevices of the bedstead, along the edges of the sacking, and in every hole or corner that can harbour these vermin; also the palliasses may be washed with it, and the floors; this not only destroys the living insects, but dries up the eggs quickly. In houses much infected, it should be applied frequently, and the floors always washed with salt and water. No damp will arise from this.

RECOMMENDATIONS FOR HEALTH.—If of bilious habit, avoid taking beer or ale, or much sugar and butter; and if feeling ill, take in time half-a-teaspoonful of grated rhubarb, and one tea-spoonful of magnesia rubbed smooth in a teacupful of water; avoid drinking much through the day; and if hungry, eat a dry crust.

Headaches are mostly the result of an overloaded stomach. If castor oil is ordered, take it in cold water.

Never kneel on the bare stones, or ground, or floors, without a mat; many white swellings have been brought on by this.

FOR TOOTHACHE.—Use a pennyworth of camphor, dissolved in half-an-ounce of spirits of wine; if this does not stop it, add a little laudanum.

A great help to refreshing sleep is to wash the feet every night, summer and winter, in slightly warm water.

FOR A COLD.—Take a cup of gruel every night after going into bed, with two teaspoonfuls of spirits of sweet nitre in it.

FOR BURNS.—Immediately apply cotton wool or wadding; keep it free from air.

FOR A GATHERING ON A FINGER.—Make a finger-stall of oil silk, wet a rag, tie round the finger, place the silk over, take at the same time a teaspoonful of milk of sulphur, in a little milk, for three successive mornings.

W. H. Collingridge, City Press, 1, Long Lane.

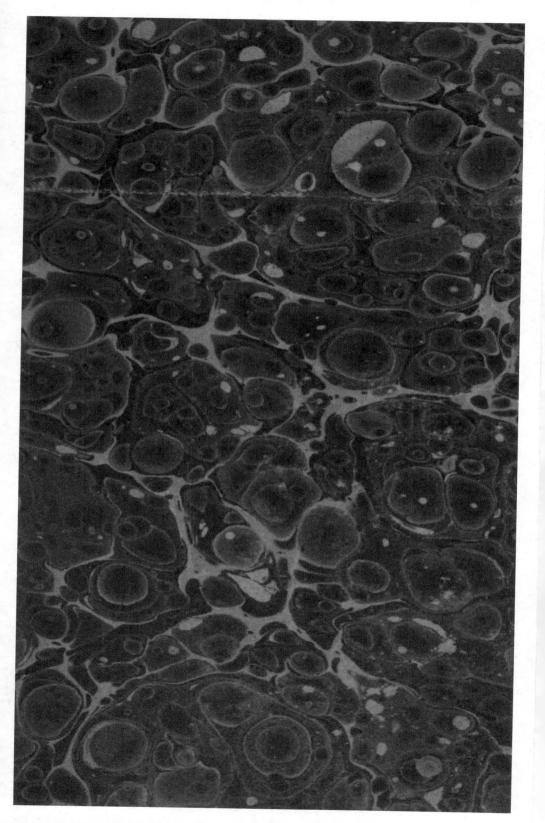

Check Out More Titles From HardPress Classics Series In this collection we are offering thousands of classic and hard to find books. This series spans a vast array of subjects – so you are bound to find something of interest to enjoy reading and learning about.

Subjects:
Architecture
Art
Biography & Autobiography
Body, Mind &Spirit
Children & Young Adult
Dramas
Education
Fiction
History
Language Arts & Disciplines
Law
Literary Collections
Music
Poetry
Psychology
Science
…and many more.

Visit us at www.hardpress.net

Im TheStory

personalised classic books

JANE
'IN'
WONDERLAND

LEWIS
CARROLL

"Beautiful gift.. lovely finish.
My Niece loves it, so precious!"

Helen R Brumfieldon

⭐⭐⭐⭐⭐

UNIQUE
GIFT

FOR KIDS, PARTNERS
AND FRIENDS

Timeless books such as:

Kids

Alice in Wonderland · The Jungle Book · The Wonderful Wizard of Oz
Peter and Wendy · Robin Hood · The Prince and The Pauper
The Railway Children · Treasure Island · A Christmas Carol

Adults

Romeo and Juliet · Dracula

Highly
Customizable

Change
Books Title

Replace
Characters, Names
with yours

Upload
Photo for
inside page!

Add
Inscriptions

Visit
Im TheStory .com
and order yours today!

CPSIA information can be obtained
at www.ICGtesting.com
Printed in the USA
BVHW040248120819
555626BV00016B/4539/P

9 781318 695317